TSUNAMI OF GRACE AND TRUTH

HEALING FOR AMERICA'S DARKNESS

"... *Jesus full of grace and truth (John 1:14).*

JOHN LINDSAY SADLER, JR.

Copyright © 2024 John Lindsay Sadler, Jr.

All rights reserved. No part of this book may be reproduced, stored, or transmitted by any means—whether auditory, graphic, mechanical, or electronic—without written permission of both publisher and author, except in the case of brief excerpts used in critical articles and reviews. Unauthorized reproduction of any part of this work is illegal and is punishable by law.

ISBN: 979-8-89419-394-6 (sc)
ISBN: 979-8-89419-395-3 (hc)
ISBN: 979-8-89419-396-0 (e)

Because of the dynamic nature of the Internet, any web addresses or links contained in this book may have changed since publication and may no longer be valid. The views expressed in this work are solely those of the author and do not necessarily reflect the views of the publisher, and the publisher hereby disclaims any responsibility for them.

One Galleria Blvd., Suite 1900, Metairie, LA 70001
(504) 702-6708

DEDICATION

I dedicate this book to the one I have lived life with for forty-nine years; a wonderful lady, my wife Lee. Her encouragement and support for me throughout our forty-three years of ministry has been priceless. She is a tremendous Bible teacher to women and she has taught women's classes in all the churches I've served. I praise the Lord for the grace and forgiveness we have shown each other in all the years we have walked together.

ACKNOWLEDGEMENTS

First and foremost, I would like to thank Susan Smith, an English professor, for her time on editing my book. She was truly a blessing to work with.

Second, I praise the Lord for the men I have heard and learned under. These men listed have helped me create this book through their wisdom of scripture and insightfulness of our world condition. These men I thank whom I have read and I've sat under their teaching: Francis Schaeffer, Chuck Colson, John Piper, R.C. Sproul, Albert Mohler, Edmund Clowney, and Os Guinness.

MY ACKNOWLEDGMENT TO THE LORD

I acknowledge that I am a wretched sinner saved by grace. God sovereignly chose and predestined me before the foundation of the world. In His time, He called me to be justified by the blood of Jesus Christ to remove the penalty of my sin. Through the Holy Spirit and the Word of God, I am being sanctified to neutralize the power of sin in my life. Then at His appointed time, He will glorify me to eliminate sin forever in my eternal life. Praise be to the Lord!

INDEX

Abounding Grace 5
Absoluteness of the Truth 8

Building Upon the Word
   of Grace 11
The Bible is the Truth 14

Common Grace 17
Church – The Upholder
   of "True-Truth" 20

Drawn to the Throne
   of Grace 23
Discovering the Truth 26

Equipped for Ministry
   by Grace 30
Evaporation of the Truth 33

Free Gift of Jesus
   through Grace 36
Freedom in the Truth 39

God of All Grace 42
God of Truth 45

Humbleness Receives
   Greater Grace 48
Holy Spirit of the Truth 51

Identity from Grace 55
Indoctrination in the Truth 58

Justified by Grace 61
Joy in the Truth 64

Koinonia (Fellowship)
   from Grace 68
Knowledge of the Truth 71

Law Submits to Grace 74
Lack of the Truth 77

Multiplication of Grace 80
Morality and the Truth 83

Never Nullify the Grace
　　of God 86
Nation of the Truth 89

Only by Grace is Someone
　　Born Again 93
Overcomers for the Truth 97

Presence of God at the
　　Throne of Grace 100
Practice of the Truth 103

Qualified to Preach the
　　Grace of God 106
Quandary Around
　　the Truth 109

Riches of God's Grace 112
Reconstruction of the Truth 115

Sufficiency of God's Grace 118
Suffering for the Truth 122

Testifying to the Gospel
　　of God's Grace 126
Tolerance of the Truth 130

Unity in the Church
　　Through Grace 134
Universality of the Truth 138

Victory in the Future
　　by Grace 142
Voice of the Truth 145

Wisdom from the Grace
　　of God 148
Weight of the Truth 151

X-Factor in Christianity
　　is Grace 155
X-Factor of the Truth 158

Yearning to Give Thanks
　　for Grace 161
Yearning for the Truth 164

Zenith of Grace is Jesus 168
Zenith of the Truth is the
　　Resurrection 171

INTRODUCTION

"Tsunami of Grace and Truth:"
Healing for America's Darkness.

John 1: 14 – "And the Word became flesh and dwelt among us, and we have seen His glory, glory as the only Son from the Father, full of grace and truth."

The sun has set on America, and most people don't realize they have settled in the darkness.

A tsunami, with its huge ocean waves, will change the landscape of any coastline it crashes. Probably one of the worst tsunamis to punch onto any shore was the India coastline. On December 26, 2004 around eight o'clock in the morning, there was an earthquake with a Richter reading of approximately 9.2. This devasting earthquake unleashed skyscraper size waves reaching eighty to hundred feet in height. This horrific event killed around 228 thousand people in fourteen countries. It was said by many to be one of the deadliest natural disasters in recorded history. Likewise, America needs a tsunami of grace and truth to be hurled over our sinful lives and the liberal and Marxist ideologies that far-left viewpoints bring to the table.

Introduction

Liberal government leaders have used the word "freedom" from the U.S. Constitution to mean that anyone can do whatever they want, even that which is ungodly. For example, "reproductive rights" of women to have such control of their bodies that they can kill a life that has been produced in their womb or outside the womb. The 2024 Democratic National Convention (DNC) celebrated joyfully their willingness to kill babies. In fact, they provided a mobile abortion site outside of the convention hall. The dark side proponents have slapped God in the face with their lack of feelings towards the unborn. The National Right to Life estimates around sixty-four-million murdered to date. Our nation has returned to the Old Testament practice of sacrificing their children to the god Molech (Jeremiah 32:35). Since God is the Creator of life, U.S. politicians have shaken their fist at God, as if they are wiser.

How about the energy issue? The climate change or "Green New Deal" is pushed on society from fear of the planet being destroyed. News flash! There is enough factual evidence to prove that this philosophy is not true, and it is designed to control and have power over citizenry. The energy issue is at stake from climate regulations. Our Creator has given the United States a bountiful supply of oil and propane to be unearthed. Using our resources will lower living expenses across the board. Again, God is Lord of all, including the weather.

Another "dark side" of America is that parents do not feel they have the freedom to guide their children's decision-making process. Public school systems have been given the freedom. Many schools adopted or are in the process of adopting curriculum that teaches children they can change their gender if they feel like they want to, but they do not teach children that their gender is perfect, as it's God given, as it is. This had led children to a desire to "transition" themselves from one gender to another, which has led to many confused and psychologically unhealthy children who believe they have the power to undo what God has perfected in them to withhold life changing information from parents that might allow their child to transition – that is to change their gender. Raising children is the parents God given right.

Finally, open borders are giving freedom to all who cross our borders without being vetted. God has created borders for nations, and the government has the freedom to deny entry to anyone who refuses to follow our laws. The teachings of God about a nation's borders are irrelevant when we allow our nation to be overrun by just about every nation on the planet. To date, approximately, twelve million have come unvetted to America according to the latest Pew Research report.

The sun no longer shines on America, and we have settled in the darkness. Yes, many don't even know the light is gone. Those who still live in the light are caught in the wake of those diminishing in darkness. People's hearts are turned away from true freedom in Christ because they love their sin.

To overcome this liberal to Marxist belief system and the sins of people in America, the Christian community must live by grace, and hopefully, the Lord will be gracious to this land. That He will allow the sun to shine on America once again. Followers of Jesus must depend on God's undeserved favor daily. We must acknowledge that everything we have comes from the gracious hands of God. The government must not be seen as our god, but Jesus Christ must be recognized as our God and Lord. God's grace is abundant, and it flows from the Lord without ceasing. However, if America holds to the godless ideologies of liberal-woke thinking, sinful living, and turns to Marxism, God's grace can be withdrawn or withheld from our nation. We will languish in this darkness without keeping God center.

Not only are we to have a tsunami of grace upon our land, but one of truth as well. As someone said and has been repeated by others, "Truth is the first casualty of war." America is in a war of philosophies; who is telling the truth? The inspiration of this book is for the reader to have the courage to speak out for truth. As Dietrich Bonhoeffer said, "Not to speak is to speak. Not to act is to act." I believe America is in

Introduction

a tail spin. If Christians don't choose to be the influencers of truth, America will crash in a sea of lies. Jesus said we must stand up for truth, for He is the Truth (John 14:6). Even though some form of persecution will come, we are to fight for the truth. The question before us, are liberal ideas and woke policies true? Are Marxism viewpoints the truth that we are to live under? Is having the freedom to satisfy all our fleshly desires really true freedom?

My book analyzes twenty-six Scripture verses about grace and truth. These verses tackle the problem we have in America, and the solution to our problem. My prayer is that this book will help the reader to have the courage to stand up for truth. Maybe, just maybe, the sun will shine on America again, and many won't have to settle in the darkness. But it will take a tsunami of grace and truth from the Lord Jesus Christ. He is "full of grace and truth" (John 1:14c) or "grace upon grace" (John 1:16). His tsunami will change the landscape of a person's heart and the ideas of America.

The majority of texts are from the ESV Bible and the information come from sermon notes and books I've read over forty-three years of ministry. Blessings to you as you read the pages of grace and truth. May a tsunami come soon to bring healing to our culture!

ABOUNDING GRACE

"Now the law came in to increase the trespass, but where
sin increased, grace abounded all the more"
(Romans 5:17-20).

Do you realize, when we were conceived that we were pride babies? That's right. In our mother's womb, we were sinners. Adam's sin guaranteed it. When we were delivered from the womb, we joined a chaotic and confused world with the certainty of death and Hell forever lingering before us. The natural action is to trust the birth status, a selfish independent nature which is our pride. Pride is at the heart of sin. As we grow from infants into adults, our pride flourishes as well. You and I have felt that being the boss in life is most satisfying and thrilling. Pride is a two-sided coin. Heads - the devil wins, and tails - we lose. There is the pride of boastfulness. Look at what I have accomplished. The applause, kind words, and pats on the back fuel this side of pride. One begins to think he has the world by the tail and that he is somebody. On the other side of pride's coin is self-pity. Poor little me! Life is not fair. Sad face and negative words can draw a crowd every time. People like pity parties because they can share their pitifulness.

Prideful adults continue to grow and develop physically, and then a crisis surfaces, and from that, many rush to temporary relief that only harms them more. Sometimes the crisis is anticipated; other times the crisis arrives in the wake of sin. Whichever way sin hits home, sin will shatter the heart, and when the heart is devastated, dreams evaporate, and hope is diminished. To be rid of sin's consequences of depression and defeat, many rush to alcohol, drugs, sex, materialism, entertainment, or isolation to escape embarrassment and heartache. Little do they realize their life will become even more broken.

When Jesus was in the womb of Mary, He was perfect, holy, and sinless. Here was God in the flesh coming into His creation to save sinners. Many of the prideful say they don't need saving, or they keep trying to fix their lives in futility. Never the less, Jesus went from the cradle to a cross to shed His blood for all who would believe that Jesus's blood covered their sins. He came to correct what Adam had done. The result of the Adam's fall is original sin. He was told not to eat from the tree of the knowledge of good and evil. Doing so allowed sin to engulf every life. But Jesus came to restore righteousness to all who would believe in His death, burial, and resurrection according to the Scriptures (I Corinthians 15:4), and all who would confess their sin. In other words, He exchanged the regenerate's sin by being sin so that righteousness could be credit to the new believer's life account (2 Corinthians 5:21).

This is amazing grace. Grace that abundantly abounds and overwhelms. God's grace is tsunami grace. When a tsunami strikes land, the landscape is changed. Similarly, when a tsunami of grace bursts onto a heart, the person will be regenerated. Regeneration of the heart allows the individual to see their sin, recognize God's holiness, and to believe in Jesus through faith. Grasping this, the person will repent and turn from sin to accept the free gift of righteousness. I heard someone say, "faith is the fruit of regeneration," and it is!

Grace is receiving what one does not deserve. All deserve to be left in their sinful prideful nature to taste death and eternal Hell. As sin increases, grace abounds all the more. The focus text expresses God's love flowing through His grace to any hardened sinner. Grace is the key to unshackle the chain of sin that burdens a life.

You may ask, "Why would God save me after all the wrongs I have done, and how I used people to satisfy my pleasures?" The Prodigal Son, who squandered his portion of his father's inheritance, experienced grace (Luke 15). His father, who was looking for his return, threw him a homecoming party. Likewise, Zacchaeus, the chief tax collector (Luke 19), was showered with God's grace. His conversion changed his heart to give back half to the poor and give back four- fold to all he had cheated. As you see, grace abounds to the worst of sinners. So, no matter how you have abandoned God in your life, or how much you have sinned, God's grace abounds. Take the thief on the cross next to Jesus on Calvary's Hill, Jesus told him that he would be in Paradise with Him (Luke 23:39-43). He had done nothing for the kingdom of God, but upon His confession he would be saved forever. This offer still stands from Jesus today to everyone who calls on Him.

When one hears the internal call of God, that person will come to Jesus. Many hear the external call, but the internal call is an effective call by the Holy Spirit to bring the individual willingly into the kingdom of God. The old nature of sin has been transformed into a nature of godliness and holiness. This is grace demonstrating how overflowing and powerful it can be.

The one who chooses to follow the Holy Spirit will now live in the Light, Jesus Christ. And His light overshadows the darkness that people were living in, and the darkness our country is in. As I stated earlier, yes, grace abounds, and when grace overflows it is like a tsunami crashing onto one's heart, and changing the landscape of the heart of sin into one of righteousness. Give all the glory to the Lord!

ABSOLUTENESS OF THE TRUTH

Therefore, Pilate said to Him, "So You are a king?"
Jesus answered, "You say *correctly* that I am a king. For this
I have been born, and for this I have come into the world, to
testify to the truth. Everyone who is of the truth hears My
voice." Pilate said to Him, "What is truth?" And when he had
said this, he went out again to the Jews and said to them,
"I find no guilt in Him (John 18:37-38).

"Without truth we are all vulnerable to manipulation."
Oz Guinness, (*Time for Truth:* . . .) (NASB 1995).

The battle in America's culture today determines who tells the truth. Like Pilate, people ask what is truth? Is CNN or Fox News telling their audiences the truth? Which newspapers are telling the truth? Is everyone spinning the story or facts to satisfy their moral or political views? Are Democrats or Republicans telling the truth? I am sad to ask this, but which church is telling the truth; churches that hold to the inerrancy of Scripture or those who do not?

For a society to flourish, absolute truth, not truthiness, must be woven into the culture's fabric. Otherwise, everybody is susceptible to being maneuvered towards the loudest voices.

Jesus is the Truth, not a truth. He came to give an anchor of absolute truth. The Truth came from outside of this world to give His creation a clear road map of life. No sideroads, exits, dead ends, expressways, but a narrow path of the Truth of how to have satisfaction in life (Matthew 5:6, 6:33, 7:24-27). However, like Pilate, it is foreign to most to say there is absolute truth. Consequently, the culture is scratching its head trying to figure out who is telling the truth.

Jesus is the Truth (John 14:6). He stated, "For this I was born and for this I have come into the world, to bear witness to the truth" (John 18:12). The truth problem is solved through Jesus Christ. He is the One broadcasting TRUTH.

Everyone has to answer these questions about creation, the fall, and redemption respectively:

1. How did it all begin? How did I come into existence?
2. What happened? Why all the chaos in the world?
3. How can it be corrected? Who can put it back together?

The answer to creation, the fall, and redemption is found in Jesus. All things were created by Him and for Him (Colossians 1:16). Sin came into the world through the disobedience of Adam and Eve which has created a chaotic world (Genesis 3). To correct the fall of man, God came into the world in the person of Jesus Christ (John 1:1, 14). He came to pay for our sin debt by nailing our sins to His cross (Colossians 2: 13-14).

Which is true to answer these basic questions regarding creation, sin, and redemption: Is Jesus, the absolute Truth or is it Satan? The devil can twist truth (truthiness) to manipulate others towards unbiblical lies. Truthiness is a belief or assertion that a particular statement is true based on how certain people perceive it, without any thought whether the statement is fact, logic, or has any good evidence. The Bible is on trial. Is the Bible absolutely true or does it only contain truth? Many on the liberal wing of theology believe the first eleven chapters of the book of Genesis is a myth, and that it is based on truthiness. Consequently, the origin of creation is through the "Big Bang Theory." Sin is reduced to the point that humankind is not sinful, and that humans are not very good sometimes. Redemption is simply someone saying they are sorry; plus, God is all about love. One can see the divide between biblical truth and man's liberal view of the three basic topics of Scripture.

Francis Schaeffer said in his 1981 speech at Notre Dame, "Christianity is not a series of truths in plural, but rather with a capital 'T.' Truth about total reality, not just religious things. Biblical Christianity is Truth concerning total reality and the intellectual holding of that total truth and then living in light of the truth."

Pilate's question, "What is truth?" was a statement of frustration, He was at a point of giving up hope of finding truth. Jesus told Pilate what truth is before he made his exasperated question, "What is truth? Jesus stated, "You say that I am a king, for this purpose I was born and for this purpose I have come into the world-to bear witness to the truth. Everyone who is of the truth listens to my voice" (John 18:37). All, who hear and obey the voice of Jesus knows the Truth, and they will not fall prey to the manipulators. For they know the truth about God as given to them in Scripture. This is the age we live in today. People say this is true because I said it. So, whatever is true for you is truth, and whatever is true for me is truth. Both might be at total opposite ends of their truth statements.

There has to be absolute truth. If not, then anybody can believe anything. For example, some people go as far to say they feel they are an animal, a different color, or a different gender. Because they believe this, then it must be true, and they want everyone to acknowledge their truth. This is where we are in society. Maybe by God's grace, we will hold to the absoluteness of truth as given in the Bible.

BUILDING UPON THE WORD OF GRACE

> "So now, brethren, I commend you to God and to the word of his grace, which is able to build you up and give you an inheritance among all those who are sanctified" (Acts 20:32, NKJV).

Who has your ear? Who influences you the most? People don't just live; they live out their philosophy of life. It may not be in a formal written statement, but their view of life is written on those who have their ear, then their mind and heart. Really, men and women don't rule, but their ideas govern their actions and behavior.

In context of the text, the Apostle Paul departs from Ephesus with a joyful sadness. He had labored three years faithfully teaching God's word to the Ephesian church. His final words, words of warning were that false teachers would try to worm their way into the church. Just so long as their agenda would be accomplished, they would not care who they hurt to gather a following. In other words, Paul is saying that he has taught them one view of life, and now others will come in to give instruction on a different view of life. So, who will they believe, Paul or the new instructors? Will they build their life upon the Word of grace or upon words of men? Which view will build for them a solid future?

The text creates a flash back of what Jesus said at the conclusion of His powerful sermon, the Sermon on the Mount (Matthew 5-7). In chapter seven, He asks where will you build your life – on sand or on rock? If you abide in the words or teachings of Jesus you build your life on solid rock. Nothing can destroy the life. On the other hand, building on sand is one who does not listen to or obey the teachings of Jesus. The life will be destroyed and it will be horrific (Matthew 7:24-27).

In our culture who is telling the truth? Who is really trying to build your life? The universities across America? The churches that dot our landscape that do not embrace the inerrancy of Scripture? The political leaders who try to sway you or manipulate you to follow their agendas?

Paul wrote to the church in Colossae warning them "not to be held captive" or "carried away" by the philosophies of this world (Colossians 2:8). Adolf Hitler was right when he stated, "If you tell a big enough lie and tell it frequently enough, it will be believed." We must listen with spiritual ears to unearth a lie. Who can you trust? The Word of grace or the words of others?

The Word of grace can build a solid life. The foundation of the Word is a living Word (Hebrews 4:12) that will tell you the truth about yourself. The truth – you are a sinner in need of a Savior. The truth – without an anchor of Truth, can easily manipulate individuals. The truth without God in the equation of life, makes everything meaningless (Ecclesiastes 12:13). The Word of grace is living because the Author is living. The author is Jesus – the Word of God (Revelation 19:13).

The Word of grace tells of your past as well. You are saved by grace and what you did in the past has been covered by the blood of Jesus. Your rap sheet is torn up, your debt has been paid, the Judge's (God) verdict is "Not guilty, justified!" (Colossians 2:13-15).

The Word of grace not only addresses your past and present life, but it tells you about your future life. No, not about a retirement strategy, but about an eternal home. The Word promises a bright future where there is no death, pain, tears, suffering (Revelation 21:1-5). John was instructed to write this down because "these words are true and faithful" (v5).

Too many Christians hardly open their Bibles. Consequently, they "drift" away from the teaching of the Word (Hebrews 2:1). It is like going to the beach. You set your beach gear and umbrella at a certain spot, then you enter the ocean. The current causes you to be pulled away from your original spot on the beach. This is what happens when we don't read and apply the Word to our lives; we are pulled away from truth.

Another factor related to our not obeying the Word is "doubt" (Hebrews 3:15). We stop believing that the Word is true and accurate. Instead of holding fast to the Word, some believe astrology, horoscopes, or palm readers.

Not only are some drifting away from hearing the Word or doubting the Word, others are "dull" in hearing the Word (Hebrews 5:11). I am almost deaf in my left ear. Listening only with that ear, I can barely make out what a person is saying to me. Likewise, some don't hold to the truth of the Word, thus they become dull in hearing. The Holy Spirit is quenched (I Thessalonians 5:19) in bringing meaning and application to the Word.

In each case, obedience to the Word is missing. If you drift from the Word, doubt its truth, or become dull in hearing the Word, you will not grow in your faith or even come to faith. To the degree we read and study the Word of God, we grow in faith, which is our sanctification.

Oh, beloved, dust off your Bibles, take them off your nightstand, and read the living Word from the living Author – Jesus. Build your life on a biblical foundation of God's grace.

THE BIBLE IS THE TRUTH

"You are near, O Lord, and all Your commandments are truth.
The sum of Your word is truth, and every one of Your righteous
ordinances is everlasting" (Psalm 119: 151, 160).

We must "be utterly convinced that there is a biblical perspective
on everything – not just spiritual matters,"
Nancy Pearcey – *Total Truth*

All truth must begin with God. We capture His truth through the Bible. There is the worldview of life, and then there is the Biblical or Christian worldview. The two views have clashed over centuries, but only one can be correct.

Not surprising, the inspired Word of God states it is truthful. "You are near, O Lord, and all Your commandments are truth. The sum of Your word is truth, and every one of Your righteous ordinances is everlasting" (Psalm 119: 151, 160). Church is not about traditions or worship styles, but about whether or not the Bible is inerrant and trustworthy. Albert Mohler, President of Southern Baptist Theological Seminary, in Louisville, KY, writes the following from his book, *Feed My Sheep: A Passionate Plea for Preaching*:

> Luther tried to go back to the first century and understand the essential marks of the church, and the first mark he listed was

preaching. Where the authentic preaching of the Word takes place, the church is there, he said. By contrast, where it is absent, there is no church. No matter how high the steeple, no matter how large the budget, no matter how impressive the ministry, it is something other than the church.

Due to the varied and colored views of Scripture, there is confusion over which church is teaching truth. For example, one church teaches women can be pastors, or instructs the gay lifestyle community that God created their sexual orientation, and another church does not. Some churches teach 'Theistic Evolution," and other churches hold to the "Intelligent Design" instruction. Which church tells the truth? As I cited in my last chapter, the Bible is under attack. The true church, as Mohler described from Martin Luther, is the one that views the Bible as total truth, and this is preached from the pulpits.

In my first church, a young man went off to college, and he entered into the gay lifestyle. His parents called and asked me to visit their son on campus. I scheduled a meeting with the student. During our time together, the biblical view was presented of why homosexuality is not in agreement with Scripture. He listened intently, but upon finishing my argument, he simply said, "Pastor, I talked to an Episcopal Priest, and he said it was fine to live this way." In seconds, my apologetics went up in flames.

Theologians, pastors, and teachers have exercised theological gymnastics to twist the Scriptures to appease a movement or a worldview. The Church's biblical authority has been silenced. Sadly, the folks that come against the Bible are the same people who never read the Bible. The reason they don't read the Bible is because they have not been born again. They have no relationship with Jesus. Yes, this includes a host of people who are members of a church. I served a church who thought more of the church's "Procedural Guide" than they did of the Bible. They could give you page number and paragraph of any issue that was on the floor of a business meeting from "The Guide." However, they could not cite a biblical text to support their argument.

Also, we must ask who is telling us the truth, the Bible or the culture? The reason is that our culture has overtaken biblical revelation. For thousands of years, the Word of God has stood the test of time. However, in America, human reason has become the idol of the land. The anti-biblical individuals can live as they choose. If necessary, they will lie, spin facts, and say or do whatever is necessary for their agendas to come to fruition. Again, this is truthiness - speaking and living without any factual undergirding.

More times than not, when churches and so-called Christians muffle the Bible, their speech blends into the culture's voice. Thus, Scripture is no longer a player in any argument. The church's teachings and the Christian's voice become a faint whisper. As mentioned, the most popular topics that create a divide between churches are women pastors and the homosexual "marriage" union. I believe these churches who support these two areas no longer remain a true church. These churches have blended into the culture, and they have allowed the culture to override Biblical truth. Consequently, truthiness has infiltrated society's thought process more than the trustworthiness of Scripture.

As Nancy Pearcey wrote, "Be utterly convinced that there is a biblical perspective on everything – not just spiritual matters," Sadly, there are only a few churches and Christians who are convinced.

Common Grace

"... For he makes his sun rise on the evil and on the good, and sends rain on the just and on the unjust" (Matthew 5:45).

Matthew 5:20 is the key verse in understanding Jesus' Sermon on the Mount (Matthew 5-7). "For I say to you, that unless your righteousness exceeds the righteousness of the scribes and Pharisees, you will by no means enter the kingdom of heaven." The religious rulers of Jesus' day didn't consider an outcast worthy of prayer. Jesus' parable explains their outlook. Also, He spoke this parable to some who trusted in themselves that they were righteous, and despised others: "Two men went up to the temple to pray, one a Pharisee and the other a tax collector. The Pharisee stood and prayed thus with himself, 'God, I thank You that I am not like other men—extortioners, unjust, adulterers, or even as this tax collector. I fast twice a week; I give tithes of all that I possess'" (Luke 18:10-14). Jesus teaches that our righteousness has to be totally different than the Pharisees and scribes.

These religious leaders were enthusiastic evangelists. They would go out of their way to convert someone to their religious beliefs (Matthew 23:15). Not only were they evangelistic, but they knew the Old Testament Scriptures (Read Matthew 23). They were adherents to the Law of God. In fact, they created some 613 laws of their own to keep the Ten Commandments and other teachings from the Old Testament. This is why they were torn out of their frame when Jesus healed someone on the Sabbath. A third religious marker of theirs was tithing. Jesus rebuked them for this because they tithed but neglected the weightier matters of the law: justice, mercy, and faith (Matthew 23:23). Jesus rebuked their faith because it was about their achievements and notoriety. They didn't recognize God's common grace upon their lives. Pharisees were duty bound, trying to work their way into God's good graces.

We too, like Jesus, are to love the sinner. Love those who are against us to show that we are indeed sons of God. These religious leaders could not do this. They were blinded by their so-called good deeds and pseudo faithfulness to the Law of God.

Unlike the Pharisees, as a son or daughter of God, you have received "special" grace. Grace that regenerated your heart to see your sin and the holiness of God. Prior to that blessing, you received God's "common" grace. Other than salvation, you received all the benefits of life like a believer. You might have good health, prosperity, a wonderful family, and a vocation that you enjoy. All of these blessings flow from the hands of God's grace. But you don't recognize the genesis of the blessings because you have not received God's "special" grace – salvation. This is what the text highlights, that the sun and rain both are enjoyed by the just and unjust.

Most, like the Pharisees, don't realize the bounteousness of God in life. All that one has is from the hands of God. King David reminds us of God's kind and generous heart in his prayer. The people had brought all the material to him for the temple to be built. From their act of faith, David prayed: "Both riches and honor come from You, and You rule over all, and in Your hand is power and might, and it lies in Your hand to make great and to strengthen everyone" (I Chronicles 29:12). David's eye of faith was opened to the greatness and generosity of the Lord.

Do you have an eye of faith to see that all that you have comes from God? It was not your mental capacity, ingenuity, or education that has brought you blessings. No, it was God's common grace. The Apostle Paul understood this point. He was a blue blood Pharisee, well educated, and enthusiastic about the Law. His conversion (Acts 9) opened his eye of faith to understand that it was God's grace that works in his life. Paul said. "But by the grace of God I am what I am, and his grace toward me did not prove vain; but I labored even more than all of them, yet not I, but the grace of God" (I Corinthians 15:10).

Thus, Paul had nothing to boast in expect in Jesus Christ. When one is blinded from faith, all the glory goes to the individual. Salvation faith sees God's common grace, the person understands it was God working in their life all the time.

Beloved, you might not understand this, but God is blessing you in so many ways. Even in your seasons of heartache. Pray that God will open your eyes to see His handiwork of grace in your life. Then He will receive all the glory and honor He created you do give Him.

Church – The Upholder of "True-Truth"

". . . if I delay, you may know how one ought to behave in the household of God, which is the church of the living God, a pillar and buttress of the truth" (I Timothy 3:15).

"If I profess with loudest voice and clearest exposition every portion of the truth of God except precisely that little point which the world and the devil are at that moment attacking, I am not confessing Christ, however boldly I may be professing Christ. Where the battle rages, there the loyalty of the soldier is proved, and to be steady on all the battlefield besides is mere flight and disgrace if he flinches at that point."
Francis Schaeffer

Late Christian apologist, Francis Schaeffer, termed truth, "true-truth," to communicate that truth was absolute not relativistic. When the Truth is voiced in culture, the Truth causes untruth devotees to coil like rattlesnakes to strike back. Why? Their humanistic influence is being threatened. Humanism teaches that man is the measure of all things. The Church has been designated by God to represent the kingdom of God who is the measure of all things, not humanism. As the late Chuck Colson stated, "The Church is to make the invisible kingdom of God visible." The kingdom of God is a kingdom of absolute truth. Truth makes the kingdom of God visible.

Kingdom of God people have been transformed to acclimatize to their new residence through their repentance of sin and their faith in the substitutionary atoning work of Jesus' cross and His resurrection. Christians have become accustomed to a new environment, the kingdom of God, by coming under the authority and rule of God. Having been acclimated to the kingdom of God life, the Church has been called to "umpire" one another in the body of Christ and the world (Colossians 3:15). In the text, "rule" means to umpire. When pseudo-truths are obvious, the church should blow the whistle to call foul. By the Lord's grace, the Church is empowered to carry out heaven's ordained task of upholding TRUTH through the power of the Holy Spirit and the living Word (Hebrews 4:12).

To young Timothy, the Apostle Paul writes the clarion call to the church then and now, "if I delay, you may know how one ought to behave in the household of God, which is the church of the living God, a pillar and buttress of the truth" (I Timothy 3:15). The Church is to be the "umpire," and support or be the foundation of the Truth. As Schaeffer stated that if the Church winks at untruth, then the Church is not confessing Christ. With that said, are churches that endorse same sex relationships and are silent on the abortion issue really churches? If the Church does not uphold the inerrancy and the trustworthiness of Scripture, is the church the church?

Our country is in a truth war. The battle is fierce and the casualties are increasing. In light of the war in the land, the Church has lost her wartime identity in the culture. All the churches that dot the landscape in America are to be fortresses of the Truth. Sadly, the Church is composed mostly of swimmers being swept away by the ocean's undertow of lies moving them away from the truth.

Most churches have sheathed their weapon, the Word of God. They have abandoned the Truth for a social agenda and liberal philosophical sermons, which pull the Church into the powerful undertow of the culture's pseudo-truths. Yes, many worship and praise the God of creation and salvation they don't even know. Thus, they leave worship believing all is right in the land.

If churches do not change their passive identity of being a sanctuary of lies, instead of a bastion of truth, America will be turned over to human reason. This will slam the door on "true-truth." Eventually, America will become a dry and barren land, because the Word of the Lord has not been a buttress of truth by churches. Amos 8:11 reads, "Behold, the days are coming," declares the Lord God, "when I will send a famine on the land - not a famine of bread, nor a thirst for water, but of hearing the words of the LORD." Schaeffer's words have sadly come true: "Where the battle rages, there the loyalty of the soldier is proved, and to be steady on all the battlefield besides is mere flight and disgrace if he flinches at that point." Too many churches have "flinched at many points," which has caused what Amos said thousands of years ago to come true, "there is a famine in the land of hearing the words of the LORD."

Drawn to the Throne of Grace

"Therefore let us draw near with confidence to the throne of grace, so that we may receive mercy and find grace to help in time of need" (Hebrews 4:16).

In your time of need, where do you turn? Most look to personal effort to alleviate pain. In *The Problem of Pain*, C.S. Lewis explains that if all is well, self-will never surrenders in the human spirit. The reality of life is that everyone will experience "pain" at some level. Yes, doctors can give relief sometimes, but even they don't have answers to many illnesses. Financial experts can offer strategies to remove the weight of debt, but cannot control the habits of free-lance spenders. Marriage counselors can give insight into marital problems, but they cannot change a heart of unforgiveness. In these situations, and in many others, most grasp self-will, even in dire circumstances. Plus, many think they don't deserve help from anyone.

The author of the book of Hebrews offers a solution of how individuals can discover comfort in their season of pain. He says to "draw near with confidence to the throne of grace" (Hebrews 4:16). Instead of running to personal effort for relief, he says get closer to God. As people come to God, they come with boldness or confidence. That is with an attitude of trust in the Lord. In other words, believing that God - "got it!" The sovereign hand of God has gripped you tightly for your good and His glory.

The "throne of grace" is where you find undeserved favor from God. Here at His throne you find goodness, kindness, peace, and joy. His love overflows you and now in your unwanted situation, you can sleep like a baby on the sovereign pillow of God's grace.

Also, the writer of Hebrews reveals that one will benefit from receiving 'mercy.' Mercy is not receiving what we deserve. Mercy is God's kindness towards the believer. Everyone needs the twin gifts of grace and mercy. C.S. Lewis also writes in *The Problem of Pain*, "God whispers to us in our pleasures, speaks in our conscience, but shouts in our pains: it is His megaphone to rouse a deaf world for the sufferer to submit to the will of God." Pain should force us or at least encourage us to look to the Lord in our pain, and then submit to His care, compassion, and yes, even salvation.

A theme in Hebrews is that Jesus is our High Priest – a High Priest Who is alive and active in a believer's life. In addition, previous to the focus verse, Jesus can sympathize with all of our weaknesses. He understands!

These gifts of grace and mercy are given to help in God's time, not our time. The end of Hebrews 4:6 is translated, "grace for a well-timed help" (John Piper). "Help" because grace and mercy aid. "Well-timed" because our High Priest on His throne delivers our help in perfect time. In John 11, Mary and Martha were upset with Jesus because their brother Lazarus was dead and buried. They told Jesus if He had been there, their brother would not have died. Being dead four days, Jesus stated that He was glad Lazarus was dead so that they might believe in Him.

God's timing is two-fold: first and foremost is for His glory. For example, the man born blind from birth. The question was who caused this blindness: the man's sin or his parent's sin? Jesus told His disciples neither sin caused it. This happened so that the works of God can be revealed through the blind man (see John 9).

Second, God does this so that you will believe that He is indeed the Son of God. One of the major themes though the gospel of John is the deity of Jesus. There are seven major miracles from turning water to wine (John 2), to the last miracle of raising Lazarus from the dead (John 11). Each of the seven were designed to reveal that Jesus is God.

In our suffering or need of help, we must hear His voice through our pain. Our self-sufficiency, self-will, or pride muffles the "megaphone" of God. We must hear the voice of God because He is shouting for us to draw near to His throne of grace and receive relief from our pain. There is no need to be chained to our suffering or pain. Be thankful out of obedience, that we have a place to run to in our pain. The attitude that we have when leaving the throne of grace is gratitude. Gratitude breaks the chain of anger, pride, resentment and leads to a place of freedom. Be free! Draw near to God! Have confidence that the Lord will help in your well-timed need.

Discovering the Truth

"Many will follow their sensuality, and because of them the way of the truth will be maligned;" (2 Peter 2:2).

"Man's love of truth is such that when he loves something which is not the truth, he pretends to himself that what he loves is the truth, and because he hates to be proved wrong, he will not allow himself to be convinced that he is deceiving himself. So, he hates the real truth for the sake of what he takes to heart in its place" (St. Augustine, *Confessions*).

God has already created all things, and humankind is on a journey of discovery of how things function and how life progresses. Discovering truth creates a culture of the Truth. Science, medicine, philosophy, inventions, and biblical truth are all based on discovery. The conclusion is that nothing is created but discovered. I had a science professor in my first church. He was quick to share that scientist are really on a journey of discovery. Through the power and leading of the Holy Spirit, the follower of Jesus, as he grows in faith, discovers the truths of Scripture. Once discovered, he obeys the truth for the glory of Jesus. Paul writes in I Corinthians 10:31, "So, whether you eat or drink, or whatever you do, do all to the glory of God." For example, when you discover from the Word of God, you learn that you are to give sacrificially to the workings of the kingdom of God, and you begin to give for the glory of God.

Our culture, though, is a pseudo-truth manufacturer. Our culture teaches that the end product of a truth is created around one's opinion, which is solidified through feelings, desires, or experiences. It matters not if there are no legitimate facts to back the opinion; the outcome is politically correct (PC) verbiage and lifestyle. It isn't PC to say, "Merry Christmas" in the public square; one has to say, "Happy Holiday." When America's Supreme Court in June of 2015 bulldozed traditional marriage, it established a cultural truth based on, in part, the weight of public opinion. When there is no biblical worldview, the humanist view of the world can be decreed by the powerful or influential.

This is what Peter states in 2 Peter 2:1. He reveals that there will be many false teachers. These teachers will hold to their so-called truth which will blaspheme or malign the truth. Saint Augustine argues that people believe their truth even if they know their truth is false. Augustine writes, ". . . he will not allow himself to be convinced that he is deceiving himself. So, he hates the real truth for the sake of what he takes to heart in its place."

The second United States President, John Adams, stated, that America's government can only succeed if the populace is moral and religious. America was founded on Judeo-Christian beliefs. This belief system is found inscribed throughout the buildings and monuments in Washington, D.C., our nation's capital. *The Declaration of Independence* states, "We hold these truths to be self-evident, that all men are created equal, that they are endowed by their *Creator* with certain unalienable Rights, that among these are Life, Liberty, and the pursuit of Happiness." What is missing in our society is the "endowment of their Creator." Government has taken over the responsibility of being the Nation's God/Creator. Consequently, babies are killed in and out of the womb. Life is not valued in the United States when someone can be shot and killed for athletic shoes or when students can desire the elimination of the Jewish population and act on that desire. "Liberty" is lost for not being able to pray in front of an abortion clinic. "Pursuit of Happiness" is strangled by high taxes, and the support of the radical climate change proponents. Radical politicians with far-left ideas, like not drilling for oil, are paralyzing our energy production which is causing prices of goods to increase. The pursuit of the American Dream has faded away.

As stated, "many will follow their sensuality, and because of them the way of the truth will be maligned;" (2 Peter 2:2). If everything is relative, based on one's opinion from his desires or experiences, then any idea, lifestyle, religious, or political thought can become a truth. What the Apostle Peter wrote centuries ago applies to twenty-first century people. In our government, there are politicians who are false teachers and leaders. As stated, they will not hold to what is true and right, because their motivation is to maintain their power, so they lie to the public. A glaring example are the "open borders." Leaders have said the borders are closed. But anyone can see this is not true through the statistics of millions of migrants who have invaded America.

What isn't addressed in cultural relativism is human sin. The selfish independent nature of each person really desires to be on stage. As I stated earlier, pride has a boastful side and a pitiful side. The boastful use power to manipulate. The pitiful actors have a suffering attitude that tugs on the heart-strings of others. The homosexual community, the immigration issue, and other social issues all shout, "Poor pitiful me; it's not fair."

With pride on the heart's stage, the logical conclusion is that anyone can produce a truth. Desires, feelings, and experiences are the factory workers to create satisfaction, and an acceptable view of oneself. A pseudo-truth comes off the factory assembly line packaged to say, "I'm right." So how many new pseudo-truths will be fashioned this year from the cultural truth factory? Remember, anything manufactured has a shelf-life. The false truths will eventually fade, especially when

America is in bondage by the government or by another nation. Then people will dig to discover golden nuggets of the Truth.

America needs to lay down the burden of needing to be politically correct. The truthiness factory needs to be closed, and Jesus needs to be on stage. He is – the TRUTH.

Equipped for Ministry by Grace

"Since we have gifts that differ according to the grace given to
us, each of us is to exercise them accordingly: . . ."
(Romans 12:6).

"As each one has received a special gift, employ it in serving one
another as good stewards of the manifold grace of God"
(I Peter 4:10).

". . . for the equipping of the saints for the work of service,
to the building up of the body of Christ; . . ."
(Ephesians 4:12).

Grace, God's undeserved favor, gifts His followers or disciples, with a variety of gifts for the good of the body of Christ (I Corinthians 12:7). In other words, every Christian has a responsibility in the church to exercise their gifts. Christians are not pew sitters; soaking in the ministry of the church without participating within the fellowship of believers. Members of a church are not in their respective church just to vote on issues. No, they are there to meet the needs of others in the love of Christ through their giftings. I'm amazed that so many Christians have a 'Burger King' mindset – "Have it your way." The church is not designed for a member's way, but for God's way and design.

The Ephesian focus passage has the word "equipping." The word "equip" is a medical term that means to put in its proper place. If you break your arm, a doctor sets it back in the proper place. God ordained before the foundation of the world that Christians are to do good works (Ephesians 2:10). Jesus stated that Christians are to be the light of the world so that the followers of Jesus can shine their good works before others (Matthew 5:14). Please understand that good works are not credit points to earn one's salvation, but they are indicators of one's salvation.

Christians are equipped (put in their proper place in the body) with different gifts to serve one another to build up the body of Christ. Once Christians find their place in the church, they have a delight in their being a part of the fellowship. Their hearts are filled with gratitude, which is expressed in the action of thanksgiving. The thankful action is ministry.

How do Christians discover their gifts? One has a passion for a ministry that God places on the heart. Then one learns the ministry and grows in the ministry. In other words, one educates himself in an area of ministry. Sometimes it is trial and error before one has a peace about a ministry. But once the Holy Spirit assigns your designed ministry, there is great joy in walking with the Lord. God's grace equips believers for delight to serve Him for His glory and honor.

There are five "F's" to help you know and to discover you are in the place God desires for you:

1. *Faith* in what God is calling you to do. I think I have a desire to do a certain ministry. I will trust God's grace in the desire. Sometimes the Lord will close this door to only open another door of ministry.

2. ***Feedback:*** Do I hear that others are benefiting from the ministry? There should be positive feedback for the ministry.
3. ***Feelings:*** Do I have joy in doing this ministry? This is key. Do I look forward to the opportunity to serve?
4. ***Fuel*** for the ministry is the Holy Spirit. Trusting the Holy Spirit to equip you as you are trained for this ministry is essential. Do not act on your own strength.
5. ***Fruit*** is ripening; Am I improving in what God has called me to do? I should be more confident, and I should see lives changed through the ministry.

In my life, my dream was to be a college basketball coach. I played the sport in high school and college. After graduating college, I started teaching. During my first year God called me into His kingdom. I was saved! As I grew in my faith, I felt the Lord was calling me to preach. Then a year or so later I came to a crossroads. I received a call from the athletic director from my high school to see if I would have an interest in coaching the varsity basketball team. My dream developed. But still, I felt I was supposed to preach. After prayer and discussion with my wife, I turned down the coaching position to learn to coach saints. After a rough start, in which one person said I would never make it as a preacher, I became a preacher for the glory of the Lord. He gave me the ability because I stuttered somewhat and He took that away. Over years of ministry, I could see the five F's above come into play. Until I had health problems, I preached for forty-three years.

Once the Lord reveals your giftedness, He equips you, and places you in the body for the good of the body of Christ. Have faith, follow the Holy Spirit's leading, listen for feedback, be fueled by the Holy Spirit, and give the Lord praise for the fruit that you are producing for His glory. Serving the Lord is a joyous experience. Hopefully, you will have that experience in your ministry.

Evaporation of the Truth

"For the time is coming when people will not endure sound teaching, but having itching ears they will accumulate for themselves teachers to suit their own passions, and will turn away from listening to the truth and wander off into myths" (2 Timothy 4:3-4).

"The sleight of the tongue has the Truth vanishing before our eyes." Unknown

"Let the lie come into the world, even dominate the world, but not through me." Aleksandr Solzhenitsyn

The sleight of tongue from liberal, humanistic, relativistic thinkers dominates America's truth base. The slick talkers of pseudo-truth or truthiness will eventually cause the demise of America because the influence of these few has usurped the Truth. Consequently, complicity of the people will be expected and enforced. The Truth is fading away in all cultural arenas. For example, the pseudo-truth advocates, the government, and liberal churches have supported the mandate that the public-school systems must teach evolution. In addition, children are taught that transgenderism is an accepted lifestyle, and the children have must sort out feelings of which gender they want to be. Homosexual indoctrination is also in the educational pipeline. The vanishing of the Truth extends from the tender age of a kindergartener through college. The twisting of the Truth has kept the unborn life in jeopardy. The church has lapsed into a theological coma allowing "true-truth" to disappear. When the Truth is abandoned, the most formidable voices will change the landscape. As history has proven, the liberal thinker will lead to bring America to the brink of a Marxist ideology – a movement towards socialism that could evolve into Communism.

The Bible teaches that the Christian is not to be carried away or held captive to the philosophies of the world (Colossians 2:8). Scriptures warn the church that there are false teachers. The time has come in our culture that many want teachers to "tickle their ears" with thoughts that make them feel good or align with their philosophy of life. As Paul said to young Timothy, many will turn away (truth evaporated) from the truth to myths. I'm amazed at the number who leave the Baptist denomination for Mormonism. The Christian denomination holds to a grace alone, faith alone salvation; whereas, Mormonism believes in a works righteous salvation. Works righteous salvation plays into one's feelings of the American work ethic that spells over into one's religion. Plus, there is a reminder not to worship idols (I John 5:21). That is to break the first of the Ten Commandment to place something before the face of God (Exodus 20:3). An idol can be your family, vocation, money, sports, and yes, even your religion. In light of the current culture's worldview, how does the Christian worldview proponent respond to those who are working to evaporate the Truth from the American society? We must stand for biblical truth! But we have to realize there is a cost.

From the teachings in the beatitudes, the Christian response is obvious (Matthew 5: 2-12). Basically, Jesus instructed that when you take the Christian character into the culture, a crisis will occur. The crisis will result in persecution from proclaiming the name of Jesus, that He is the only way to heaven (John 14:6). Even though suffering will come with the Truth, the Christian's motivation is to make "true-truth" reappear like a rainbow after a rain storm. Isn't it interesting that you can mention Buddha, Muhammad, or Confucius, in a conversation, but when Jesus is mentioned a silence or stare appears.

Criticizing the nation won't allow the Truth to reemerge in America. The transformed life gives the Christian grace in the battle of ideas to combat the false teachers. The Apostle Paul writes, "to speak truth in love, (Ephesians 4:15). To young Timothy, he writes, "with gentleness correcting those who are in opposition, if perhaps God may grant them repentance leading to the knowledge of the truth," (2 Timothy 2:25). Jesus and Stephen as they were taking their last breaths said, "Forgive them for they do not know what they are doing" (Luke 23:34, Acts 7:60). Early in His ministry, Jesus taught that His followers are to "love your enemies" and to "pray for those who persecute you" (Matthew 5:44).

If the Truth is our treasured possession, and we want the Truth to resurface in our land, then all Christians need to cease living a fragmented or a compartmentalized life. The Christian community must heed Solzhenitsyn's statement, "Let the lie come into the world, even dominate the world, but not through me." The Christian must speak and live the Truth in the land of lies with boldness, but also be wrapped in an attitude of agape love.

FREE GIFT OF JESUS THROUGH GRACE

"But the free gift is not like the transgression. For if by the transgression of the one the many died, much more did the grace of God and the gift by the grace of the one Man, Jesus Christ, abound to the many" (Romans 5:15).

"For if by the transgression of the one, death reigned through the one, much more those who receive the abundance of grace and of the gift of righteousness will reign in life through the One, Jesus Christ" (Romans 5:17).

"The Law came in so that the transgression would increase; but where sin increased, grace abounded all the more, so that, as sin reigned in death, even so grace would reign through righteousness to eternal life through Jesus Christ our Lord" (Romans 5:20-21).

Christianity answers a huge life question: How can I get to heaven? Every religion outside of Christianity answers the question through works. They make the death of Jesus on the cross and His resurrection a sham. To those, the love-work of Jesus is meaningless because the Cross and the empty tomb are not enough to secure one's salvation. The life equation for eternal life is Jesus alone + grace alone + faith alone = eternal life. Salvation is a gift. If I must work for it, salvation is no longer a gift. Jesus declared on the cross, "It is finished!" (John 19:30). Salvation is complete for all who will believe in Jesus.

Receiving something free is hard for many to accept. It is hard to comprehend that folks who leave the Baptist church run to works-based faiths. All works-based faiths don't understand grace. In America, we have a pull ourselves up by the boot straps mentality. This bleeds over to a religion that teaches we have to work to maintain salvation.

Even decision making is a form of works. Look what I did: I walked down an aisle, I was baptized, I tithed, I went to church, and I served on committees. None of this will get you into heaven. Regeneration is instantaneous. God transforms your heart, that is your nature, and gives you the faith to believe and to repent of your sins. Regeneration precedes faith and repentance.

Salvation is all the work of God in a life. It is like the "Golden Chain of Salvation" states: those whom He foreknew (from the foundation of the world; not looking down the corridor of time), He predestined, those He predestined, He called, those He called, He justifies, and those He justifies, He glorifies (Romans 8:29-30). This is the work of God. Instantaneously when you are saved, you are regenerated in a simultaneous way and are given faith to repent of your sins.

The elementary question for those who hold to a work-based salvation is how much work is enough to please a holy God? When you die will your record show you did enough and who will decide if you did enough? I asked a Muslim waiter in a restaurant how he would be saved? He raised his arms in the shape of scale. He said, "If my good deeds are more than my bad deeds, I will go to heaven." One's earthly walk is not one of peace, but of being weighted down with the basic question – how much more do I have to do to satisfy God? It would be cruel of God to move the goal line continually or increase the quota of good works each year. In retail business, the boss always increases the

Free Gift of Jesus through Grace

amount of sales for the sale person's goal each year. That would be a most frustrating job, not to mention an exasperating life.

Jesus set the goal line at the Cross. Here is your free gift. In fact, Jesus states that He will give you the grace to have faith (Ephesians 2:8-9). Faith is something one cannot muster. Through Adam sin entered the world. All have sinned or missed the mark. But where sin increases, grace overflows greatly to give the one with faith a position of righteousness. "The Great Exchange" is when righteousness is credited to you because Jesus exchanged your sin for God's righteousness. In other words, Jesus became sin for you and took all your sin on the cross, and imputed to you the righteousness of God (2 Corinthians 5:21).

You don't earn righteousness, it is God's free gift to you through your being justified before Him. You have been justified through grace (Romans 3:24), through faith (Romans 3:28, 5:1), and through the blood of Jesus (Romans 5:9). What's missing in this list? WORKS!

Now, let's be clear, Christian's do works to show their faith, but not to earn their salvation. James in his letter makes this crystal clear. Faith without works is dead and one is justified by his works (James 2:24f).

Maybe the reason you are working so hard to satisfy God is because your heart has never been regenerated? Ask the Lord to change your heart, and if He does, the work of a satisfaction quota will be met. Now you can serve the Lord out of a heart of delight not duty; and to display that you are a believer in Jesus. Not to earn Jesus' favor, but to show your gratitude by working for His glory (I Corinthians 10:31).

Freedom in the Truth

"If you abide in My word, you are my disciples indeed. And you shall know the truth, and the truth shall make you free" (John 8:31-32)

"Truth without freedom is a manacle (shackle), but freedom without truth is a mirage." Os Guinness, *Time for Truth* . . .

From the Garden of Eden to now, humankind was designed to live within certain boundaries. God told Adam and Eve not to eat from the tree of knowledge of good and evil for they would die. When they believed Satan's lie that they wouldn't die, they learned death is a certainty, birth pain is a reality, and making a living is a labor of intensity (Genesis 3:16-19). When we are free to fulfil our wants, desires, and emotions without the guard rails of the Truth, then sin has its freedom to make life miserable. St. Augustine wrote, "Man is only free to sin." Until one is born again, or regenerated, that person will always live out his sinful nature. All who are born from above will still sin. But when a spiritual transformation occurs, that person will no longer practice sin. I John 3:9-10 states, "No one born of God makes a practice of sinning, for God's seed abides in him, and he cannot keep on sinning because he has been born of God. By this it is evident who are the children of God, and who are the children of the devil, whoever does not practice righteousness is not of God, nor is the one who does not love his brother."

In today's culture, the Truth has little or no freedom to be expressed without opposition by a liberal church goer, or a leftist politician that controls the country. Jesus challenged the Pharisaical religious position. His freedom to teach the Truth was shut down by them. So much so, they argued for and won His crucifixion. In America today, people of the Truth are stifled or handcuffed by being tagged as irrelevant, foolish, narrow-minded, and worse. Isn't ironic, that those who hang on to their pseudo-truths, think freedom is in killing a baby, transitioning a child's gender, and controlling the climate. In truth, God created life, He assigned each a gender, and He completely controls the weather.

Many teenagers yearn to be free from their parents' rule. Then in adulthood, they quickly learn that their freedom is limited. They are bound to the laws of the land, the requirements of their employer, and if married, the responsibilities of a family. Laws are broken, slackness occurs, or finding a new workplace is found, and an affair or divorce are all escape actions from feeling restrained. These young adults feel unfulfilled. This is why the divorce rate is high, suicides have increased, and there are more substance abuse cases that lead to various addictions. These young people are looking to be free. True freedom, Guinness writes is expressed through historian Lord Acton, "Freedom is not the power of doing what we like but the right of being able to do what we ought." From adolescence to adulthood, a spiraling of sin can occur through "freedom," but happiness through true freedom comes from doing what is right.

Jesus made it clear where freedom originates, "If you abide in My word, you are my disciples indeed. And you shall know the truth, and the truth shall make you free" (John 8:31- 32). There are two factors in abiding in the word. One, you prove to be a follower, a student of Jesus. Second, freedom is found. The guard rails of life are in the Bible. These Biblical guard rails bring freedom.

In John's second epistle, he rejoices that many are walking in truth by keeping the commandments (2 John 4-6). Likewise, in 3 John, he again is elated that God's children are walking in truth (vv3-4). Then in verses 9-12, he compares Diotrephes with Demetrius. Diotrephes is not walking in truth but in his fleshly pride; whereas, Demetrius has a good testimony from the truth. One is free, the other tries to be free in himself. Everything outside of Jesus is sin and places one in bondage. Without the Truth there is no freedom and humankind can only live out of their sinful flesh. The realization is that there is no true freedom without the Truth; there is only an imagined desert oasis where freedom is lost in pseudo-truths.

The Truth gives security, significance, and satisfaction. Staying within the designed playing field of life creates a sanctuary. The boundary lines are drawn by the Word of God. By staying within the boundaries, significance is created from within. One knows that the Lord is pleased and glorified. When security and significance lock arms, then satisfaction of life wells up within the person. All of this occurs because the Truth is free to complete its work.

Many think they have pitched their tents in a beautiful desert oasis, then one day they will realize, it is just sand. How tragic!

GOD OF ALL GRACE

"After you have suffered for a little while, the God of all grace,
who called you to His eternal glory in Christ, will Himself
perfect, confirm, strengthen and establish you"
(1 Peter 5:10).

Most people don't see or understand the grace of God. God revealed His grace when creating the universe and world (Genesis 1-2). Everything – the world and all humankind - created was perfect. Then from the disobedience of Adam and Eve (Genesis 3) sin entered into the world. Their and our **s**elfish **i**ndependent **n**atures have created chaos and suffering. Amid our chaotic world, God's grace is displayed towards every human life (see chapter on Common Grace, p. 17). God's main characteristic is holiness which consists of love and wrath. God desires to shower His goodness on humanity. This is who He is. He cannot do anything less. God just operates from His nature. As Peter wrote, God is the God of all grace. Understand that everything you possess flows from the grace of God. The grace of God is an everlasting flow of goodness toward us. God's grace can be compared to flowing rivers, or the rays of the sun. Each continues daily to provide refreshment and warmth.

Sadly, most people don't acknowledge God's grace or favor in their lives. It is the person's strength, intelligence, and self-motivation that receives credit for the individual's accomplishments. Because their nature is sinful and self-righteous, they cannot help but express themselves this way. Even though people promote themselves, Jesus knows their hearts and minds are far from Him. This is why Jesus when crucified cried out, "Forgive them for they know not what they do" (Luke 23:34). Stephen who was stoned expressed the same cry (Acts 7:59-60). The Apostle Paul simply stated that he was "ignorant" of the things of God and that was why he was a blasphemer and persecutor of Christ (1 Timothy 1:13). Similarly, most are like toddlers who are too ignorant to understand why they can't do something when told "no" by their parents. The people's ignorance is why Jesus was persecuted two thousand years ago. The persecution of Jesus continues today because people today are too unenlightened to see the goodness of God toward them. What love God has for His creation. Even though most don't acknowledge God, He continues to shower blessings upon everyone through His common grace.

Peter's text also addresses suffering. Even in suffering God bestows His grace upon the sufferer. Suffering is multicolored in that it ranges from physical to spiritual. In the letter of 1 Peter, he addresses those who suffer for Christ. Like in Peter's day Christianity in our culture is no longer relevant. When you have a people who are ignorant of God, they cannot tolerate those who see God as relevant.

In America's culture, the progressives socialist end game is for Americans to be dependent upon the government. The State becomes the god of the people. The threads of a God centered nation that have held America together are slowly being cut away from the fabric of our country. The thread of the family has been pulled away as well. The identity of a family is clouded today. Prayer in public is withdrawn from the culture; the desire to remove "In God we Trust" from currency is shared by many; and some also want to eliminate God in our pledge of allegiance to our flag. A woman's right to her body outweighs the life of a baby she is carrying. Allowing children to decide their gender is horrifying. Having open boarders, clamoring about climate change, and reducing the nation's energy supply, all these and more are destroying the United States. If you stand for God shaping the framework of our country, then you are marginalized in society. One is tagged as ignorant, stupid, narrow minded, or a bible thumper.

In spite of all the suffering that comes with standing up for God, God's grace prevails. Yes, the Christian might even suffer severely, but the Lord promises that He will perfect, confirm, strengthen and establish His followers. He will *perfect* the believing sufferer whom He has effectively called to salvation to wholeness. God will *confirm* or set fast, and He will *strengthen* or make sturdy, and finally, He will *establish* or lay a foundation in the person's life. Wuest's translation of I Peter 5:10, from Precept Austin website, reads, "But the God of every grace, the One who summoned you in Christ with a view to His eternal glory, after you have suffered a little while, shall himself make you complete, shall establish you firmly, shall strengthen you, shall ground you as on a foundation." The Lord of all grace will sustain the believer who is tempted by Satan and who suffers. These are difficult days for the Christian in America; the earthly future is not that promising for the Christian. But we must rely on the grace of God to sustain us.

God is the God of all grace. Despite the turmoil in our country, the attacks from Satan, or in times of suffering, the Christian can trust in the sovereign hand of the Lord. Each night rest your head on the sovereign pillow of the Lord, and you will sleep like a baby.

GOD OF TRUTH

Into Your hand I commit my spirit; You have ransomed me,
O LORD, God of truth (Psalm 31:5).

"You are My witnesses," declares the Lord, "And My servant whom I have chosen, so that you may know and believe Me And understand that I am He. Before Me there was no God formed, and there will be none after Me (Isaiah 43:10).

The introductory or focus Scripture texts proclaim two facts about God:

First, He is the God of truth. Second, He is the only true God. Each of these attributes is hard to digest. His statements of truth are in His living Word, the Bible, which gives a living hope from the living God. The Scriptures direct us to creation, which points us to God's truth. Old Testament books reveal the Holy attributes of God as a most loving God and a God of wrath. God is a triune God: Holy Father, Holy Son (Jesus), and Holy Spirit. God the Father **selects** or plans His kingdom residents, God the Son redeems, purchases, or **saves** the kingdom citizenry, and God the Holy Spirit secures, preserves, **seals** the kingdom populace (Ephesians 1:1-13). God's kingdom consists of those who have come under His authority and rule. One knows that he is part of the kingdom of God by his love for God (Luke 10:27), and his obedience to the Word of God (I John 3:24).

David in Psalm 31 reveals his belief that the Lord is the only true God and a God of truth. David sinned by committing adultery or rape with Bathsheba, and he had her husband, Uriah, killed on the front lines in a battle. The prophet Nathan brought David to his knees to repent by telling him through a story that David was the man in the story. Nathan told him that the Lord had forgiven him, but his son from Bathsheba would die (2 Samuel 11-12). David mourned his son's death, but he said he would see him again. Here was a man after God's own heart that called on the rock of his salvation – God (Psalm 31). David also wrote Psalm 51 which is a response to his sin as well. The shepherd boy who became king realized that what the Lord teaches is indeed truth. A host of his Psalms reflect this belief of God's truth. Yes, David was a chosen one of the Lord to lead the Israelite nation. But he as a king, like all of us, had feet of clay. The one and only true God never forsakes His elect. As we learn in David's story, there are still consequences to our sin. In Psalm 31, my favorite text is verses 14-15, "But I trust in you, O LORD; I say you are my God. My times are in your hand, rescue me from the hand of my enemies and from my persecutors." Like Isaiah, he claims the only true God and that he is trusting his spirit to the Lord.

At the center of God's truth, character, and kingdom is the resurrection of Jesus. Jesus is God (I John 5:20). Christianity has a living God. Every other faith around the globe has a god that is dead. Without the resurrection, Christianity would be 'just' another religion. Due to the fact that Jesus rose again on the third day, Christianity moves from being a religion to a relationship with God. In fact, God establishes Himself in the life of every believer. The believer is the temple of God. No other faith can claim what Christianity can and does – God is alive and He lives in the hearts of all His followers.

In a world of pluralistic faith views, which faith is telling the truth? The easy answer to the question is that all views will one day lead to God or heaven. But can that be true? Other faith gods demand a works righteousness to please the god. Each of these faiths operate out of duty.

The God of Truth desires His followers to delight in God's goodness and grace and as a result, the individual's aspiration is to produce good works. If one knows Jesus and abides in His words, then he will know the truth, and the truth will set him free (John 8:31-32). The key is to know that good works will not earn one enough credits to graduate to heaven. God's grace is the only credit needed to graduate, which comes through Jesus. Jesus made it crystal clear how to arrive in heaven; it is only through Jesus that one can come to the Father or heaven (John 14:6).

The only way one will realize that the God of Truth is the only true God is to be born again or regenerated. Good works will not create a new heart, religious traditions will not, nor will rule keeping. Only by the grace of God will one know the truth, that God is truth – God the Father, Son, and Holy Spirit (Ephesian 2:8-10).

Isaiah was correct in his text; there is no god before or after the Triune God of the Bible. David was right in declaring that God is the God of Truth. This must be pondered. How about you? Are you searching for the God of Truth, the only true God, or will you remain satisfied in your religion?

HUMBLENESS RECEIVES GREATER GRACE

"For through the grace given to me I say to everyone among you not to think more highly of himself than he ought to think; . . ." (Romans 12:3a).

"But He gives a greater grace. Therefore, it says, "God is opposed to the proud, but gives grace to the humble" (James 4:6).

"You younger men, likewise, be subject to your elders; and all of you, clothe yourselves with humility toward one another, for God is opposed to the proud, but gives grace to the humble" (1Peter 5:5).

What is missing in most Christians is the exhortation of Scripture to be humble. Paul, James, and Peter each highlight the attribute. Jesus spotlighted the characteristic as well. "For everyone who exalts himself will be humbled, and he who humbles himself will be exalted" (Luke 14:11). The problem with most folk is that they think too highly of themselves. My teenage son used to tell his friends who would be bragging about themselves, "You are not all that!" Professor, former President of Westminster Seminary, Ed Clowney wrote, "Humility springs from the total dependence on the grace of God." Dr. Clowney revealed his humility by coming to my first church and preaching. I was amazed that a seminary president would come to such a small church.

Humility should be the chief mark of our righteousness in Christ. It is in the soil of humility that grace can truly be rooted. One can't say I'm humble before God unless that person is humble towards others. Humility screams that there is no such thing as individualism. In other words, we need each other. Pride yells back and says no, you can live for yourself, and achieve goals alone. Humility embraces others, prays for others, encourages others, hopes the best for others, and even forgives others.

Again, Jesus set the benchmark for humbleness. Matthew records Jesus ministry from its inception. Jesus sits while teaching His disciples and those in ear-shot the Sermon on the Mount (Matthew 5-7). He begins the sermon with the beatitudes. To follow Him one must have the character of the beatitudes. The character change needed to happen is to be born again. One must see himself as "poor in spirit" or being spiritually bankrupt. Or as one writer stated, "blessed are those whose idols are broken for theirs is the kingdom of heaven." In other words, one must be righteous before God. Only God imputes righteousness and the believer is to impart right living towards others. To be clear, God in His election process regenerates individuals according to His will (John 1:12-13, Ephesians 1:4) and the person then repents of his sin, and he then is forgiven and found not guilty.

Then Jesus teaches, "Blessed are those who mourn and they shall be comforted." What the believer mourns is his sin. But the Comforter, the Holy Spirit, who now lives within the person brings comfort. He reminds the person that he is forgiven and that the weight of sin has been lifted. Now the person still sins but does not practice sin (I John 3). The first beatitude justifies the person and the second sanctifies the individual.

Now that the person has a relationship with Jesus and his righteousness exceeds the righteousness of the scribes and Pharisees (religion) (Matthew 5:20) he mourns his sin, and now he is humbled. Pride no longer rules the heart. Position in life is no longer imperative. Possessions are scaled below their significance. Jesus teaches, "Blessed are the humble (meek) for they shall inherit the earth."

The person who exhibited great humility in the New Testament is John the Baptist. The Baptist knew his lane or purpose as the forerunner of Jesus. This is why he stated, "He must increase, but I must decrease" (John 3:30). Andrew Murray in his book *Humility: The Beauty of Holiness* wrote, "Humility is nothing but the disappearance of self in the vision that God is all." John Calvin's *Institutes* 2.2.11 writes, "But that of St. Augustine pleases me even more, 'So if you ask me concerning the precepts of the Christian religion, first, second, third, and always I would answer humility."

To reiterate Jesus' teaching … "for everyone who exalts himself will be humbled, but he who humbles himself will be exalted" (Luke 18:14). The Apostle Paul realized that all he did for the kingdom of God was through the grace of God. Plus, all that he was and would become was by the grace of God (I Corinthians 15:10).

As a follower of Jesus, we must not see ourselves as most important. We are not to look for the applause of man, or push our way to the top of our vocations. Paul wrote to the Philippian church, we are to be content where God has us in position, financially, and with talents (Philippians 4). Yes, the promise is that the humble will receive greater grace than the proud. Trust in God's sovereignty, sufficiency, and satisfaction to make a humble spirit come to fruition.

HOLY SPIRIT OF THE TRUTH

"When the Helper comes, whom I will send to you from the Father, *that is* the Spirit of truth who proceeds from the Father, He will testify about Me, (John 15:26).

"But when he, the Spirit of truth, comes, he will guide you into all the truth; for he will not speak on his own initiative, but whatever he hears, he will speak; and he will disclose to you what is to come" (John 16:13).

"We may as well face it: the whole level of spirituality among us is low. We have measured ourselves by ourselves until the incentive to seek higher plateaus in the things of the Spirit is all but gone… We have imitated the world, sought popular favor, manufactured delights to substitute for the joy of the Lord and produced a cheap and synthetic power to substitute for the power of the Holy Ghost." A.W. Tozer

"…I can't think of anything more essential for God's church everywhere, and especially in the western hemisphere where it seems that the Holy Spirit is all but missing from most of our churches." *The Forgotten God* by Francis Chan

The focus texts glean four facts. First, the Spirit comes from the Father. Second, the Spirit speaks on behalf of the Father. Third, the Spirit is a Person, and fourth, the Spirit guides us into all truth. Again, what separates Christianity from other faiths is that God lives in the believer through the Person of the Holy Spirit. The Spirit becomes the primary teacher for the student of Jesus. Everyone is taught by someone. For example, a parent teaches his children about racism. A child doesn't become racist; he is taught prejudicial behaviors. My dad corrected me harshly at age nine. We were driving with an African American fellow; I said, "George, are you a ...? I used the horrible "N" word. My dad stopped the car in the driveway, his huge hand grabbed me, and he scolded me for using that word. I had to apologize immediately. A parent can fuel the sinful nature, which causes the child to express a pseudo-truth. Or the parent can correct his sinful nature. The Holy Spirit does the same. He teaches us truth and corrects us when we do sin (John 16:8-11). This is the promise of Jesus to His disciples and to us, "And I will ask the Father, and He will give you another Helper, to be with you forever, even the Spirit of truth, whom the world cannot receive, because it neither sees Him nor knows Him. You know Him, for He dwells with you and will be in you" (John14:16-17).

Tozer and Chan expressed their concern about the Spirit not being acknowledged by most Christians. Chan's book title, *The Forgotten God*, reflects the view of most Christians and churches – the Holy Spirit is forgotten. We forget that the primary purpose of the Holy Spirit is to glorify Jesus (John 16:14) and to testify about Jesus (John 15:26). Plus, as the focus text (John 16:13) says, "He will guide us into all the truth." But to support Tozer's point, many Christians have substituted the things of the world to satisfy them, instead of the Spirit. We look to everything else but the Spirit in our time of need. Paul states in Romans 8:26, "the Spirit helps us in our weakness and He intercedes for us." He further states in Romans

8, we are to set our minds on the Spirit and not on the flesh. You see, the Spirit desires to be a prominent player in each of our lives. I believe too, we have allowed deep theological beliefs and knowledge to replace the workings of the Spirit. Knowledge is good and to have a healthy grasp of theology is important in our Christian growth. The Spirit can use all this to better enhance our Christian lives. He is the teacher of all Truth.

The gift of the Holy Spirit, the third person of the Trinity, gives believers the advantage (John 16:7) over the world, the flesh, and Satan's temptations. Having this advantage, Christians know biblical truth to discern if public opinion mirrors this truth. To discern right from wrong when the fleshly desires want to be satisfied, and when Satan throws a temptation in front of a believer knowing biblical truth keeps the believer on the path of righteousness.

The Holy Spirit acts like an umpire in a baseball game. His rule book is the Bible. Like the childhood act I did, an act that is performed that doesn't line-up with the Scriptures is what the Holy Spirit calls an "out" in the "game" of life. Every day the believer is challenged by the sinful trio (world, flesh, and Satan). This trio's goal is to convince you that lies are truth. They want your life to be depressing, unfulfilling, not satisfying, so you will always be looking for the next best thing to bring you pseudo-peace. The Holy Spirit in concert with the Word of God teaches truth. Before every action taken, every opinion expressed, or any lifestyle attraction happens, it needs to be filtered through the Word of God. Then the Holy Spirt will be the wise counselor to guide you. Because the Holy Spirit is a Person, He can be "quenched" (I Thessalonians 5:19) by believers dishonoring the Lord, which causes Him to "grieve" (Ephesians 4:30). As I said, His primary desire is to bring glory to Jesus (John 16:14).

Some faiths don't acknowledge the Holy Spirit or any spirit. Others mischaracterize Him as a force, not a Person. The resurrection expanded the Holy Spirit's work in the Old Testament to every person and just not to leaders. In addition, Jesus' teachings of the promise that a Helper would come to testify to the Truth (Ezekiel 36-37).

When humankind tries to sort through information and so-called facts, the default is most always towards the sinful desire, a prideful conclusion, or the direction of one's belief system. Culture pays little or no attention to the condition of the human heart. The heart manufactures idols, pride, covetousness, and a lying spirit. John Calvin wrote, "The heart is an idol factory."

This is why Paul's letter to the Galatians is vital to understand. He tells us to walk by the Spirit, and you will not gratify the desires of the flesh (5:16). When we walk and live in the Spirit we produce fruit: love, joy, peace, patience, kindness, goodness faithfulness, gentleness, and self-control (5:22-23). All we need in life is in the Spirit's fruit. Sadly, some Christians don't realize they have this sweet fruit of life. We must yield to the Spirit in our lives and not have Him be dormant.

Most people are wandering in a desert of self-centeredness trying to discover truth. Sadly, they are looking for life's peace in all the wrong places. Peace is not within self, but beyond them in the Holy Spirit, Who desires to live within a person. The Holy Spirit has empowered all who follow Jesus, to know Truth, to share Truth, and to live the Truth. As Jesus said, when you know and abide in the truth, you will be free.

IDENTITY FROM GRACE

"But by the grace of God I am what I am, and his grace toward me did not prove vain; but I labored even more than all of them, yet not I, but the grace of God with me"
(I Corinthians 15:10).

Have you ever wondered how God allowed Saul, a persecutor of the church, to become Paul a protector of the church? Saul was born a Roman citizen to Jewish parents in Tarsus, which is modern day Turkey, in A.D. 6. He studied the Torah under Gamaliel to earn a right to become a Pharisee from 20-30 A. D. In 30 A.D. to 33, he persecuted followers of Jesus in Jerusalem and Judea. In 33 – 36 A.D., Saul was converted on the Damascus road, he spent three years in Arabia, and then began preaching Jesus as the Messiah as the Apostle Paul.

Behind the curtain of Paul's timeline is God's grace. This is why Paul stated, "I am what I am by the grace of God." On the Damascus road and during his so-called seminary years was when the curtain was opened for him to realize the grace of God. It was God's sovereign favor on Paul's life before the foundation of the world that he learned. Paul wrote in Galatians 1:15, "But when it pleased God, who separated me from my mother's womb and called me through His grace." It is a mystery of why God allowed, then Saul, to persecute the church prior to his conversion. This seems to be the strategy of God to take the broken and use them for His glory. Turn the bible pages to the Old Testament and you find Moses, David, a prostitute Rahab, and other broken sinful people who God used to advance His kingdom.

As one writer described grace, "There is nothing you can do to make God love you more and there is nothing you can do to make God love you less." John Newton, former slave trader, wrote the infamous hymn, "Amazing Grace," that begins, "Amazing grace how sweet the sound that saved a *wretch* like me." Like Paul, when God regenerates a person's heart, that person realizes how wretched and wicked is their heart. Jeremiah 17:9 provides truth: "The heart is deceitful, wicked, incurable above all things, who can know it?" The depravity of sin should never be taken lightly. There is no escape from a depraved life unless God's grace unlocks the shackles of sin in your life. Saul was bound to his sinful action of persecuting Christians. He was receiving accolades from his co-conspirators for his grievous work. He received all the glory for his ministry of persecution.

When salvation came to Paul, he realized who he was. Doctor Luke writes of what Paul said of himself, "But I do not consider my life of any account as dear to myself, so that I may finish my course and the ministry which I received from the Lord Jesus, to testify solemnly of the gospel of the grace of God" (Acts 20:24). Paul wrote in First Corinthians that he labors harder than most, not him but the grace of God working through him. The heart of his ministry was to tell others about what he experienced – the grace of God. To do that, he said his life was only valuable to fulfill the call upon his life to preach "the gospel of the grace of God." This was why Paul is deemed, "The Apostle of grace," as Luke stated.

Paul's identity was wrapped up in the grace of God. From his spiritual birth through his earthly ministry, he knew he was to proclaim God's undeserved favor upon his life. Thus, he writes, whether you eat or drink, whatever you do, do all for the glory of God (I Corinthians 10:31). His old life was for his glory; his new life was for God's glory.

Is your identity packaged in your vocation, family, education, etc. or is it in the grace of God? Do you receive glory for who you are, or do you let the Lord receive all the glory? Have you abandoned your life to Jesus, so you can finish faithfully the race He has set before you?

To be clear, we are what we are by the grace of God. From our birth to our salvation, all happens by the grace of God. All the work we do and all we have is by the grace of God. The life we have is a life of grace, nothing more or less. It is all grace!

Josiah Conder (1789-1856) highlights this text through his hymn, "My Lord I Did Not Choose You:"

> My Lord, I did not choose You,
> For that could never be.
> My heart would still refuse You,
> Had You not chosen me.
>
> You took the sin that stained me,
> Cleansed me, made me new;
> Of old You have ordained me,
> That I should live in You.
>
> Unless Your grace had called me,
> And taught my opening mind,
> The world would have enthralled me,
> To heavenly glories blind.
>
> Chorus:
> My heart knows none above You,
> For Your rich grace I thirst.
> I know that if I love You,
> You must have loved me first.

INDOCTRINATION IN THE TRUTH

"Christians embrace a theology of the cross,
not a theology of glory" Martin Luther

". . . You shall love the Lord your God with all your heart and with all your soul and with all your might. These words, which I am commanding you today, shall be on your heart. You shall teach them diligently to your sons and shall talk of them when you sit in your house and when you walk by the way and when you lie down and when you rise up. You shall bind them as a sign on your hand and they shall be as frontals on your forehead. You shall write them on the doorposts of your house and on your gates" (Deuteronomy 6: 5-9).

The short interpretation of the focus text is to teach our households the Truth. As Luther stated, a Christian worldview is a theology of the cross, not a theology of one's glory. A theology of the cross is one that bids a follower of Jesus to come and die. To understand the Christian faith, one must die to self. Jesus was clear, if His followers wanted to find life, they had to lose their life (Matthew 10:39, 16:25). A Christian is to take-up his cross daily, deny self, and follow Jesus (Matthew 16:25, Luke 14: 25-33). As John the Baptist stated, "He

(Jesus) must increase, but I must decrease" (John 3:30). These truths we learn by reading the Bible, and by obediently applying the Bible to our daily lives.

The husband of the household is to be the spiritual leader. It is his responsibility to set the example of living out biblical truth in front of his family. As the focus text states, "you shall teach them diligently to your sons and shall talk of them when you sit in your house, and when you walk by the way and when you lie down and when you rise up." When the father talks, sits, walks, lies down, and rises up, the Word of the Lord is on his mind and tongue. The Word is foremost in his thought process.

When applying the theology of the cross to the family, parents should be diligent about teaching their children the ways of Christianity. Parents are diligent about vaccinating their children, but they are laissez-faire about how the world is indoctrinating them. Most parents encourage their children to get a liberal education, and they allow them to choose their faith belief system. A few even consent for the child to choose his gender. So many households are throwing their children into the jaws of the worldview. Bottomline: the worldview states that humankind is god, and life is to fulfill our desires. Public schools, colleges and universities, and yes, some churches uphold and teach the worldview, but the worldview should always be challenged in the home.

Solomon wrote in Ecclesiastes that the worldview is vanity, and most are just chasing after the wind. He writes about the vanity of wisdom, self-indulgence, work, and other life issues. At the end of the twelfth chapter, he concludes, the equation of life should include God – "Fear God and keep His commandments, for this is the whole duty of man" (12:13). Just the opposite, a worldview is to keep the desires of the flesh satisfied.

To reiterate, when rearing children, a family needs to attend a church that believes the Bible is inerrant, but also the parents must teach and live the Word. It has been documented that when both parents attend church, the child(ren) will more than likely not abandon the church in their teen to adult years. They teach their children that all have sinned (Romans 3:23), but Jesus died to forgive them their sins (Romans 6:23a), and to have eternal life, they are to confess Jesus as Lord and Savior, (Romans 5:8,10:9). As John Newton wrote, "Man's two greatest needs are to know that he is a great sinner and Christ is great Savior." The tragedy is either the parents rear the child in a liberal church or no church, or their walk with the Lord is either immature or they have a pseudo-faith. Parents need to show humility, grace, and love to others, and to declare the goodness of the Lord. Without parental guidance in Christian matters, many teenagers, after receiving a driver's license or achieving graduation, will never darken a church door again.

Biblical indoctrination must be a staple in a family. The book of Proverbs has been subtitled, "How to handle life skillfully." Solomon's book of indoctrination, Proverbs, fulfills the Deuteronomy 6 passage.

The Apostle John writes to the church in Ephesus (Revelation 2), who left its first love, to do the following: *Remember, Repent,* and *Return. Remember* God's goodness and grace in life. Then *repent* from not loving God foremost in life. Then *return* to Godly deeds of the faith. It is through returning to an indoctrination of the Truth that a family will discover joy and peace in life, along with a secure future. Families will see their children handling life skillfully for the glory of the Lord.

JUSTIFIED BY GRACE

"... and are justified by His grace as a gift through the redemption that is in Christ Jesus" (Romans 3:24).

Justification is one of the rings in the "Golden Chain of Salvation." Justification cannot happen unless God has foreknown you, predestined you, and then called you. Those whom God foreknew, He predestined, and those He called will be justified. Then following justification is one's future glorification (Romans 8:29-30). In the text, foreknown means that God knew you before the foundation of the world and choose you for salvation (Ephesians 1:4, I Peter 1:3, I Timothy 1:9). Foreknowledge is not God looking down the corridor of time to see who would choose Him. Those whom He foreknew, He predestined to heaven, and those He predestined, He effectively called into His kingdom through regeneration by the washing of the blood, Spirit, and the Word of God to be justified. No one can refuse the effective call of God upon their life. Theologian Wayne Grudem's, *Systematic Theology*, describes, "Justification is God's instantaneous legal act in which He thinks of our sins as forgiven and Christ's righteousness as belonging to us, and declares us to be righteous in His sight."

Justification is a one-time legal action by God to declare a person of faith, not guilty, but righteous. This is a grace action by God. He gives a person something he does not deserve. The proof of one's right standing with God is through sanctifying works. In the book of James, he states that one is justified by works (James 2:26). James does not state that one must work for salvation, but one's salvation is seen through works.

The faith God gifts a person with is to believe in the works of Jesus on his behalf. Thus, this justifies the person before God as not guilty (Romans 5:1). Being justified by faith grants peace with God through Jesus Christ. In other words, a person of faith does not have to worry about being condemned by God (Romans 8:1).

Through God's amazing grace, God showers His special grace upon a person whom is foreknown and predestined to be effectively called by faith to be justified before Him. The overflow from being justified is one's works to show that he has truly been declared righteous.

One must understand this is wholly a process by the sovereign hand of God. No one can earn salvation, be good enough to be granted a right standing before God, or be so right-standing religiously that God will accept that person into His kingdom. Jesus is crystal clear, "For I say to you, that unless your righteousness exceeds the righteousness of the scribes and Pharisees, you will by no means enter the kingdom of heaven" (Matthew 5:20). Only Jesus has allowed one's gift of righteousness to override the righteousness of the law givers.

God imputed or credited one's life account with righteousness. The classic verse is 2 Corinthians 5:21. "For he (God) made him (Jesus) who knew no sin to be sin for us, that we might become the righteousness of God in him (Jesus)." Theologians call this the "Great Exchange." Jesus took all of someone's sin, past, present, and future, and imputed God's righteousness onto the person's life account.

When I pray for lost people. I don't pray that they make a decision for Jesus or say a sinner's prayer. I pray that God regenerates the heart of that individual. That God will take the person's heart of stone and turn it into a heart of flesh. Ezekiel 36:26 is clear that this is the work of God not of any human effort or will. John 1:12-13 reiterates this truth, "But to all who did receive Him, who believed in His name, He gave the right to become children of God, who were born, not of blood nor of the will of the flesh nor of the will of man, but of God." I pray God regenerates an individual's heart so that he truly follows Christ throughout life.

A person's transformation will be evident by the desire to worship, fellowship, learn the Word of God, and to exercise works of faith. The individual's character will be changed. The person's language is godly, he displays acts of kindness, and is gentle, and has an air of peace. In other words, John the Baptist said to bear fruit in keeping with repentance (Luke 3:8).

The theological book of the Bible, Romans, declares God's justification by grace (3:24), by faith (5;1), and by Christ' blood (5:9) should give every believer a deep hope and peace as they journey towards their glorification. As one writer explains, in our justification, the "penalty" of sin is removed, in our sanctification, the "power" of sin is paralyzed, and in our glorification, the "presence" of sin is vanished. All believers experience the amazing work of God's grace. The follower of Jesus is set free from the weight of sin. The Christian stands righteous, holy, and blameless before God. There is no condemnation for the saint (Romans 8:1). Alleluia!!

JOY IN THE TRUTH

"These things I have spoken to you so that My joy may be in you, and *that* your joy may be made full" (John 15:11).

"I rejoiced greatly to find some of your children walking in the truth. . ." (2 John 1:4).

The most noticed attribute missing in the Christian community is joy. There are sad faces strained from worry and regret. One person stated that most Christians hang on a cross of discouragement because one hand is nailed to the worries of tomorrow and the other is nailed to the regrets of yesterday. Anxiousness and remorse unhinge Christians from trusting in the sovereignty of God. Thus, joy escapes them. Someone has defined joy as "having the deep settled confidence that God has everything under control." Not having this confidence in God makes one unthankful for the situation. A Christian is to be thankful in all circumstances (I Thessalonians 5:18). A thankful attitude fuels joy. This anchors the fact that He has the future in His hands. In Psalm 31:15a, David confidently rejoices, "My times are in Your hand." Plus, He has forgiven the past, present, and future sins. This fact should energize joy!

Joe Holland's article in, "Table Talk," February, 2017, describes four types of joy. I elaborate on each type, and I renamed two in italics:

1. *Fool's gold joy* from "Finding joy in sin." Enjoyment in satisfying the fleshly desires. Fool's gold joy is a placebo for satisfaction. When David took the census, he listened to Satan and not to God (II Samuel 24:10, I Chronicles 21:1) which caused his pride to overtake his trust in the Lord. David cried out that he acted foolishly. The Lord repeats numerous times to not worship idols, abstain from immoral sex acts, and obey the Ten Commandments. The truth is that sin never brings lasting joy.
2. *Fair-weather joy* is reworded from "Finding joy in good circumstances." Similarly, fair-weather fans have joy when their favorite team is always winning, but when losing, they switch from a losing team to a winning team. Joy is lost once the situation is no longer pleasant. As long as life is going in a positive direction, joy abounds. When the wind shifts, depression, dissatisfaction, and discouragement blow into the person's heart. The truth is trusting God in whatever circumstance you might find yourself in brings better results.
3. Fading joy – Joy fades when rooted in the materialistic. It is like the Word sown in the Parable of the Sower (Mark 4:1f). Great joy is given, but the weeds (things of the world) entangle the person to choke off joy. It is only a momentary feeling of happiness or contentment. Examine someone's attic, garage, or storage areas, and you will find a host of fading joy fills each. The truth is that the 'stuff' of this world will not bring lasting joy.
4. Forever joy – Forever joy flows from a relationship with Jesus (John 15:11). Here the truth promises joy in Jesus. Jesus joy creates . . .

    A. Joy from salvation (Psalm 51:8-12). In King David's life, sin has robbed him of the joy of his salvation. His sexual sin with Bathsheba, and then having her husband, Uriah, killed bankrupted him spiritually. The man after God's own heart (1 Samuel 13:14), allowed sin to steal his joy. David shares his repentance of his sins in Psalm 51. Here he is pleading for the Lord to restore to him the joy of his salvation (12a). There is wonderful joy in salvation. Our sins have been forgiven, we are clean, and stand righteous before a holy God.

B. Joy in knowing that God sovereignly has everything under control (Psalm 115:3). Psalm 115:3 states, "Our God is in the heavens, He does all that He pleases." As I stated in the beginning of this article, "joy is the deep settled confidence that God has everything under control." This brings wonderful joy to our lives. Knowing the climate in the world and our nation, everything seems to be unraveling. However, the good news, Acts 17:26, shares, "From one man He made every nationality to live over the whole earth and has determined their appointed times and the boundaries of where they live." God is on His throne and He has it all under control. We can rest in His Word!

C. Joy in being a citizen of His kingdom (Romans 14:17). The text reads, "For the kingdom of God is not a matter of eating and drinking but of righteousness and peace and joy in the Holy Spirit." The Holy Spirit gives us great joy for being in the kingdom of God. Our joy is not of this world, but in Jesus Christ who gives this joy to all who abide in Him (John 15:11). In John 15:1-11, the word "abide" is used ten times. Continuing in Jesus, who gives the kingdom to all who believe and follow Him, He promises deep joy.

D. Joy in the strength received (Nehemiah 8:10). In building the wall around the temple in Jerusalem and hearing the reading of the law, Nehemiah says, "the joy of the Lord is our strength." Strength comes from being joyful in Christ and His Word.

E. Joy in song (Nehemiah 12:43). This is one of the great statements in Scripture. "And the joy of Jerusalem was heard far away." The Lord had provided for the temple and the wall. He had given protection and strength for the wall to be completed. The people rejoiced in what the Lord had done, and their joy was heard far away. I have asked churches, "Has your community heard your joy over what God is doing in your church?" All believers and churches must sing about the following:

1. Sing with confidence in God. (Philippians 4:13, 19)
2. Sing of contentment in God. (Philippians 4:11-12)
3. Sing of complete peace "of" God and "with" God. (Philippians 4:7, Romans 5:1)
4. Sing to celebrate Jesus. (Philippians 4:4)

Jesus' truth taught that if one is grafted into Him and the person abides in His Word, then the individual would have the fullness of His joy (John 15:11). The Holy Spirit's fruit of joy (Galatians 5:22) and continuing in God's Word produce joy (John 15:1f). This is why the Apostle John wrote, "I have no greater joy than this, to hear of my children walking in the truth" (3 John 1:4).

KOINONIA (FELLOWSHIP) FROM GRACE

"For it is only right for me to feel this way about you all, because I have you in my heart, since both in my imprisonment and in the defense and confirmation of the gospel, you all are partakers of grace with me" (Philippians 1:7).

Paul, in prison in Rome for defending the gospel, had the Philippian believers on his heart because they supported, prayed, and encouraged him. Their grace towards Paul created a sweet fellowship with him. This is what fellowship does, it shows each other underserved favor or grace.

The writer of Hebrews exhorts believers not to forsake the assembling together. However, the prior verse in Hebrews 10:25 is a plea for fellowship. "And let us consider how to stimulate one another to love and good deeds" (v24). True koinonia desires for all within a church to love each other and for each person to perform acts of kindness.

In order to achieve fellowship, two things must be ongoing in a believer's life: forgiveness and compassion. A Christian must always be ready to forgive a wrong done against him. Plus, he is to respond to a need with compassion.

Someone wrote that unforgiveness is the cancer within most churches. This is one reason why so many churches have fights and why many leave a particular church. One pastor wrote about a longtime friend/elder who abandoned his church. When this occurred, the Pastor was quick to respond to his friend/elder. The Pastor did not give Satan a foothold over the disfellowship action. The breakup was not going to disrupt their friendship or the fellowship in the church. The family left, but the church continued pursuing her goals, and the Pastor remains friends with him to this day. The opposite could have happened. Bitterness, hatred, or strife could have developed. But the grace of God prevailed, and none of Satan's tactics came to fruition.

Within a body of believers there are many needs that require someone's attention. Compassion is not only heartfelt but it has hands and feet. Reading the synoptic Gospels, one finds that Jesus "felt compassion." Whether towards an individual, like a leper, or towards a crowd of hungry people, Jesus had a heart for them and reached out to them, one by touching a leper to heal him, and the other by feeding thousands by multiplying baskets of fish and bread. We are in a large church. The Life Group that we are part of creates unity by the class praying for each other weekly. When one is sick in the class, meals can be delivered to their home.

In most of my churches, I had deacons care for the congregation. I developed teams of deacons to care for those going through life difficulties. One team ministered to families with newborns and families going through a period of bereavement; still another team watched over the home bound; and a final team of deacons visited members in the hospital. Each team ministered in their area for a quarter, and then they were assigned a different area of ministry. This way, the deacon body is exposed to the variety of ministries to the congregation.

America was in the midst of the coronavirus pandemic in 2020. Even though the majority of American's carried out the mandate to "stay at home," caretakers, like doctors, nurses, and other medical personnel, were on the frontlines provided care for those who attracted the virus.

Koinonia (Fellowship) from Grace

We witnessed Samaritan Purse constructing a hospital facility in New York City. Churches provided food and other services to help those in need. Yes, the Christian community was praying for those stricken by Covid, and others put hands and feet to their prayers.

The Apostle Paul not only promoted and taught about fellowship and compassion, but he experienced both in the sweet fellowship from churches; like the one in Ephesus where he spent three years, and like the church in Philippi.

But the bedrock of fellowship is grace. Without grace, the two relational actions of forgiveness and compassion could never reach their potential. Grace's highwater mark is to glorify the Lord Jesus. This is the major responsibility of the Holy Spirit Who lives in the believer (John 16:14). When fellowship is realized it is all for the glory of Jesus and not ourselves. This is why Paul wrote, "But by the grace of God I am what I am, and His grace toward me did not prove vain; but I labored even more than all of them, yet not I, but the grace of God with me" (I Corinthians 15:10).

Koninonia flourishes when the believer does not quench the Spirit (I Thessalonians 5:19) which grieves the Spirit (Ephesians 4:30). Ephesians 4:31 describes what happens when the Spirit is grieved: "Let all bitterness, wrath, anger, clamor, and evil speaking be put away from you, with all malice." Then Paul exhorts the believer in verse 32: "And be kind to one another, tender hearted, forgiving one another even as God in Christ forgave you." This is true koinonia or fellowship in the body of Christ – the church.

Grace is working when undeserved favor is given to one another. During the famine in Egypt, Joseph, the second in command under Pharaoh, demonstrated God's grace towards his brothers who had sold him into slavery thirteen years ago (Genesis 37-50). Listen to Joseph's words of grace in verse 50:21, "Now therefore, do not be afraid; I will provide for you and your little ones." "And he comforted them and spoke kindly to them." This is grace in koinonia!

KNOWLEDGE OF THE TRUTH

"Reason is the devil's whore." Martin Luther

". . .who desires all men to be saved and to come to the knowledge of the truth" (1 Timothy 2:4).

The origin of humanity's fall came when Adam and Eve ate from "the tree of the knowledge of good and evil" (Genesis 2:17). Once that disobedient act took place, the consequence was humankind's nature was shackled to sin. The act of eating from the tree was humankind's declaration of independence from God and wanting to be like God. People can choose right from wrong, but only God has the authority to decide right and wrong. When His authority is diminished, men/women become 'god.' Humankind was created with an umbilical cord tied to God. This is why Jesus taught, "You can do nothing apart from Me" (John 15:5). When the cord was severed in the Garden, humanity staked its claim in its independence.

Humanity's self-absorbed knowledge based on truthiness has tried to stabilize differences, and correct wrongs by saying that humans are basically good. Improve the environment by giving everyone jobs, a house, transportation, health care, and education, and all will be well in the land. It is a lie! Why? The sin, selfish independent nature, of humanity is not recognized or acknowledged.

The focus Scripture text from the book of Timothy states that God desires for all to be saved so that they can come to the knowledge of the truth. Salvation from what? The penalty of sin! Jesus death, burial, and resurrection are the pathway for the forgiveness of sin. An empty cross and tomb are the highwater marks of Christianity. However, many view this text as a proof text for universalism – our love filled God desires for all to be saved. This false gospel forgets that all mankind has the responsibility to come to Jesus. When God through the power of the Holy Spirit regenerates a heart, this changes the nature of the person from sinful to righteous. Thus, the individual will be compelled (meaning of woo) willingly to come to Christ (John 6:44). Universalism is man's reasoning, not biblical truth. Luther is right that "reason is the devil's whore." Luther meant that reason cannot be divorced from God's revelation through His Word and faith. Reason divorced of these can lead someone astray, like the universalist.

Having the knowledge of the truth, knowledge of salvation, opens the eyes and hearts to the sin nature of humanity and how sinful humankind naturally responds:

- **dead spiritually** – Colossians 2:13,
- **enslaved by sin** - John 8:34,
- **governed by sinful nature, controlled by the world's system, captive to the devil** - Ephesians 2: 2-3,
- **blind** - Ephesians 4:18,
- **defiled in conscience** - Titus 1:15 -16,
- **trapped in darkness** - Colossians 1:13,
- **without understanding** - 1 Corinthians 2:14,
- **hostile towards God** - Romans 5:7,
- **a hater of light** - John 3:19-20,
- **without desire for God** - Romans 3:11,
- **without fear of God** - Romans 3:18.

These twelve sin characteristics reveal the darkness of man's soul and life. It is no wonder Jerimiah 17:9 tells us that the heart is incurable, desperately wicked, and deceitful. Only by having the knowledge of the truth that Jesus saves from the penalty of sin will someone be put in his proper place of – being a child, a sheep, and a slave of God (Luke 12:32). All believers are children of God. As I John 3 states, there are children of God and children of the devil. The child of God is righteous; whereas, the child of the devil is not. Followers of Jesus are called sheep. This is one of Jesus' favorite metaphors of describing a believer. Sheep can only see three feet, are fearful, won't drink from a running stream of water, and cannot right themselves when they are cast down in a divot in the pasture. Are we not like sheep in need of a Shepherd? Fearful, frightful, and fragile. Finally, as disciples of Jesus, we are His slaves or servants. We are called to be obedient to His Word and to abide in Him. Our lives are no longer ours. We now live for His glory, not our glory.

As I wrote in an earlier chapter, it warrants repeating, as someone wrote, the cross removes the *penalty* of sin, the Holy Spirit eliminates the *power* of sin, and glorification destroys the *presence* of sin. The insurrection of the original family, the first Adam, was only resolved by the resurrection of the second Adam – Jesus. Jesus will lead all of His followers to the knowledge of the truth or salvation.

LAW SUBMITS TO GRACE

"For sin shall not have dominion over you, for you are not under the law but under grace" (Romans 6:14).

A wife was married to a husband that was very demanding. He stipulated that she clean on certain days, place the groceries in a proper sequence in the cabinets, make the bed daily, etc. Even though burdensome, she complied to his instructions because of her love for him and fear of continued complaints from him. He died and eventually she remarried. Her new husband was kind, helpful, generous, and gracious because of his love for her. She found herself doing the things in her first marriage under a cloud of duress, now willingly doing them.

Grace empowers the believer to keep the law.

The law was a weight to live under in the Old Testament, but under grace the law is fulfilled with gladness. Due to the Israelites misbehavior or disobedience, the law of Moses was given. Even though a line in the sand was drawn by God, the Old Testament followers could not keep the law. Through a casual reading of the Old Testament, one finds the Israelites obeying after they were disciplined by God. The correction usually happened by God sending a foreign nation to capture and place the Israelites in bondage. Then they would repent, and they would find favor with God.

One, especially, finds this sinful behavior in the book of Judges. Seven times the people of God are at rest with Him; then they create idols to worship, thus breaking the law that was given to them from God by Moses. Seven times it is written that the Israelites "did evil in the sight of the Lord ..." (Judges 2:11, 3:7, 12, 4:1, 6:1, 10:6, 13:1). Seven judges or leaders were raised up to deliver the people and allow them to rest again. This is a foreshadowing of the only true Deliverer, Jesus, who would truly rescue believers from the weight of sin via the cross.

So what purpose is the law (Galatians 6:19)? Due to transgressions, the law was given. The law revealed sin and showed when it was broken. But the law cannot produce righteousness; it cannot give life and the kingdom of God (Galatians 5:21).

So how does one keep the law? Only through Jesus Christ! Jesus said He came to fulfill the law not to abolish it (Matthew 5:17). In Christ, the follower of Jesus is empowered through grace by the Holy Spirit to keep the law. In the Bible, there are sins which are transgressions (intentionally breaking the law; i.e. speed limit); iniquities (planned sin, deception to break the law; i.e. David). Only grace can break the bonds of sin.

Like the lady who was married, she desired to please her husband out of duty not delight. Christians desire not to be law breakers because of their love for God, but without grace it is still a burden and struggle. His grace allows us to fight off unrighteousness. The world with all its glamor, our fleshly desires, and the temptations of Satan (Ephesians 2:2) all are cravings to pull believers off the path of righteousness. Yes, there is a love for God but these three pillars of evil many times place a dark cloud over our love for God. But grace is sufficient to give us the victory over sin and to fulfill the law. We keep the law through delight in Jesus and not through duty.

Warning – grace doesn't give us a license to sin (Romans 6:1-2). Through Adam all have sinned. The new Adam, Jesus, gives life and freedom from sin. Yes, we all battle with sin, but Christ through our faith in Him will supply the grace needed to be victorious over sin. The law was our tutor. However, faith in Jesus removed the law from being our tutor. Galatians 3:24-26 reads. "Now before faith came, we were held captive under the law, imprisoned until the coming faith would be revealed. So then, the law was our guardian or tutor until Christ came, in order that we might be justified by faith. But now that faith has come, we are no longer under a guardian, for in Christ Jesus you are all sons of God, through faith." We are now justified by grace (Romans 3:24), justified by faith (Romans 5:1), and justified by His blood (Romans 5:9). Our right standing with Jesus makes us righteous through our justification. Praise God for our justification, our right standing with God. This is why Paul addressed many of his letters "to the saints." We are law keepers through grace because of our being saints. Rest well in Jesus saints!

LACK OF THE TRUTH

"Yes, truth is lacking; And he who turns aside from evil makes himself a prey" (Isaiah 15a NSAB 1995).

"They bend their tongue *like* their bow; Lies and not truth prevail in the land; For they proceed from evil to evil, and they do not know Me," declares the Lord" (Jeremiah 9:3 NSAB 1995).

"For the wrath of God is revealed from heaven against all ungodliness and unrighteousness of men who suppress the truth in unrighteousness. . . For they exchanged the truth of God for a lie, and worshiped and served the creature rather than the Creator, who is blessed forever. Amen" (Romans 1:18,25).

If one listens to TV talk shows like "The View," "The Talk," late night hosts (Fallon, Kimmel, Colbert), Oprah Winfrey, and others, he will hear the TV hosts claim their view is truth. Any other opinion is considered heresy to them. In fact, if Christians voice a different thought, they are considered narrow minded, fundamental, or simply crazy. If you disagree with the television celebrities, the liberal news commentators, or the far-left, progressive politicians, you become their prey. "While Paul was saying this in his defense, Festus said in a loud voice, 'Paul, you are out of your mind! Your great learning is driving you mad' (Acts 26:24). Festus, a Roman leader, thought Paul's testimony to King Agrippa could cause continued imprisonment or death (verses 30-32). But Paul said to Festus, "I am not out of my mind, most excellent Festus, but I am speaking true and rational words (verse 25). As Paul had become the prey in his day, Christians in America today are the hunted, proving the truth of Isaiah 59:15a.

In America, we have observed the hunted: a baker, a florist, conservative political figures, and others are being dragged into the truth maligner's dungeon. Jeremiah stated that lies prevail in the land. As in the prophet's day, lies have swept across the landscape of America and evil is rampant in our society. The Apostle Paul was clear that truth has been exchanged for a lie, and in our culture the creature is worshipped, not the Creator.

The dam of lies has burst, and the waters of those lies are flooding our country. Our country is flooded with the lie of abortion. Even though her body hosts another life, a woman has the right to that other life, according to our society. Even after the baby is born, she can allow the baby to die. The truth is that God creates life (Psalm 139). The gender issue says a person can change his or her gender. The truth is that God gives each person his or her gender (Genesis 2). Another hole in the dam that is flooding our country is climate change. Again, the truth is God is in control of the climate (Job 37:5-7, Psalm 135:6-7). In His controlling the climate, our God has given energy resources which can be gleaned from our land. Yes, we are to protect the creation, but also use the energy resources that God has provided for the country as well. Illegal immigrants are flooding our country through open borders. The United States government has allowed to date around twelve million to illegally come into our land. The truth is that God has set boundaries and borders for countries to be honored (Psalm 74:17, Deuteronomy 19:14, Jeremiah 31:17). America has replaced God and His Word with man's reasoning, along with a desire for power and control. With these biblical ideas that fly in the face of what's happening in America, Bible believing individuals are the hunted because they will not adhere to non-biblical thinking and ideas. Who is responsible for making holes in this dam that has caused the flooding of ideas to overflow us?

First and foremost is the church. Liberal theology - not believing that the Bible is authoritative and inerrant - has caused this flood of lies to overflow our society. The church has morphed into the culture, instead of the church transforming the culture.

Second, the family. Families have been more concerned about the material world than the spiritual. Comfort leads to conformity, which also leads to complacency. Non-biblical lived through the family flood our country with acceptable immoralities.

Third, the educational system. Education from grade school through the university level indoctrinates students with politically correct truthiness more than the basic facts in a subject area. How sad it is to hear students not know basic American history or how the world was created! The Truth of God and the Bible will not be found in the secular educational arena. Lies prevail through the halls of education because they lack the truth.

Fourth, the judicial system. From local courts to the Supreme Court, justice and righteous laws are hard to find. Legal tactics evade truth. The Supreme Court weighs in cultural opinion more than righteous thinking. About sixty years ago the Supreme Court began to reveal its hand of unrighteousness. Two prime examples are the *Engel v. Vitale* decision in 1962 and the *District v. Schempp* in 1963 decision on banning prayer and bible reading in school. Along with liberal churches and seminaries, these rulings began the erosion of righteousness in America.

These pseudo-truth court decisions drown America in unrighteousness. THINK! While many tube down the river of lies, some hold onto the life raft of the Truth – they are the hunted.

Multiplication of Grace

Grace and peace be multiplied to you in the knowledge of God and of Jesus our Lord. (2 Peter 1:2).

My son served our country through the Navy for twenty years. During his service, he taught the responsibilities of basic seamanship to the new recruits. The course was designed to help them know the workings of the ship, so when they boarded, they would be somewhat familiar with the vessel's function. However, true knowledge of the ship would not be realized until they had time to experience the everyday activities of the vessel.

Peter states that as knowledge of God and Jesus deepens, grace and peace are increased in the believer's life. The Greek word for to know the Lord is "gnosis." When the Greek prefix "epi" is added, one has the word knowledge. This knowledge of the Lord is not head understanding, but the knowledge one has from experiencing the Lord's workings in his life. This knowledge of God is more intimate and personal than simply "gnosis" or to know.

Grace is God's favor upon the believer's life and peace is the total well-being of the person. The word peace means to bind together what has been broken. That is to bring the brokenness into wholeness. The Christian grows in their relationship with the Lord as he matures in the knowledge of God. This comes through experiencing His goodness and trustworthiness by being obedient to His Word, the Bible. The Lord multiplies grace and peace as He is trusted.

To multiply means to fill or to be made full, grow, or to increase. Simply put, it means to cause the increase to become greater. Grace and peace increase in the Christian's life as the person is faithful to the Lord. "Epignosis" is to give a clear and exact knowledge. This applies to my son's teachings about seamanship. Through my son's teachings, the new sailors were given an idea of what to expect on the ship, but it became a reality when they experienced it first-hand.

People can read the Bible, know theology, but do not know the Author. Nicodemus is an example. He knew the Old Testament. He was a Pharisee, ruler of the Jews. He came to Jesus by night and he recognized Jesus as Rabbi or Teacher. Jesus, more or less, said you may know about Me, but you don't have knowledge of Me. Jesus told Nicodemus that he must be born again or born from above in order to see and to enter into the kingdom of God. In other words, Nicodemus must be regenerated, or his sinful nature changed, to come to Jesus. Unless one is born again, that person will not have the knowledge of Jesus to receive grace and peace.

Many so-called Christians are banking on their baptism, church membership, or their heritage to arrive in heaven upon death. These have religion but not a relationship with Jesus. They know about Jesus, but they don't have the deep-down knowledge of Jesus that comes from a relationship with Him. Only those who are regenerated or born again will enter into the kingdom of heaven future – heaven.

In the meantime, while believers journey towards heaven, they need grace and peace multiplied to their lives. Life is tough. Jesus never promised a life without sufferings. This is a key thought in Peter's first letter. In fact, this is a promise of Jesus that suffering will come if a Christian stands up for Jesus in the culture (Matthew 5:10-12).

But Peter gives the ultimate promise from Jesus. A promise that he experienced in his life. Grace and peace are increased when there is a knowledge of the Lord. Peter was broken from denying Jesus three times prior to His crucifixion. However, Jesus, John, and Peter had a meal together on the Galilee/Tiberias seashore (John 21). This is where Peter really began to experience the grace and love of the resurrected Jesus. But also, a wholeness was experienced as well.

Martyn Lloyd-Jones brings the discussion to a close, "There is nothing more dangerous than to have our heads packed with knowledge concerning the contents of the Bible, if that stops in the head and does not move our hearts and does not influence our will."

Psalm 43:10 adds to our closing, "Be still and know that I am God. In Hebrew, "be still" means to "let go, or to release." David simply says for the reader to let go of the sinful life in order to truly know God. It's good to know that "yada" in Hebrew has the same meaning as the Greek word, "epignosis" (or knowledge). By letting go of a self-centered, sinful life and coming to Jesus, a person will have the knowledge or experience of the multiplication of God's amazing grace.

Morality and the Truth

"Many will follow their sensuality, and because of them the way of the truth will be maligned; . . ." (2 Peter 2:2).

"Were they ashamed because of the abomination they had done? They certainly were not ashamed, and they did not know how to blush" (Jeremiah 6:15, 8:12).

The sixties saw the first wide-spread sexual revolution in America. Now almost sixty years later, comparatively, the sixties were the kindergarten era of sexual expression. Today people "hook-up" not even knowing the person's name for a sexual rendezvous. This explosion of sex has sanctioned sex with children, animals, same gender, co-habitation, prostitution, and adultery. In other words, at all cost, many believe that sexual cravings must be satisfied.

Many of these sexual acts thrive in the church, with the acceptance of same gender relationships, transgenderism, co-habitation and adultery. What these actions do is to malign or blaspheme the truth. One author references 2 Peter 2:2 from the website, "Precept Austin:"

"Peter says that because of the lascivious lifestyles of "so called saints" and "church goers", the watching world will judge the whole church based on their evil behavior with the result that the reputation of Christianity and God Himself are slandered and denigrated. Not only that, but the lost world smugly justifies (at least in their warped way of thinking) their own licentious behavior. They mock and scoff at the gospel of Jesus Christ because of nominal "Christians" who do not follow the Lord Whom they claim as Savior."

The Truth is maligned through the character of the so-called Christian and the Church. Sadly, though, neither blush. People's shame is missing when they do evil acts. No one is sorrowful when he is caught in the act or discovered. For example, celebrities and political figures whose sexual acts have been brought into the light publicly try to justify their evil actions. Shame is gone when a church places a "rainbow" banner across the front of the church. Embarrassment disappears when non-married living together couples are accepted into the church. Blushing is gone when there is no repentance from unwed mothers in a church.

What has allowed the sexual revolution to accelerate in America at warp speed? When there is no standard and people live only to satisfy their fleshly appetites. The Apostle John declares, "No one born of God makes a practice of sinning, for God's seed abides in him; and he cannot keep on sinning, because he has been born of God. By this it is evident who are the children of God, and who are the children of the devil: whoever does not practice righteousness is not of God, nor is the one who does not love his brother" (I John 3:9-10). John is clear, if one practices sin, he is not born of God. The operative word is "practice." All Christians sin. Some even fall into sexual sins. John states, "If we say that we have no sin, we are deceiving ourselves and the truth is not in us" (I John 1:8). A Christian, however, does not "practice" or habitually sin. He knows he has sinned, then he repents to cease from the evil act. The work of the Holy Spirit allows Him to bring conviction of the sin to the sinner. "If we confess our sins, He is faithful and righteous to forgive us our sins and to cleanse us from all unrighteousness" (I John 1:9).

If the Church and America continue this path of free sexual expression, then the judgement of God will come upon the nation. "As it is written in the law of Moses, all this calamity has come on us; yet we have not sought the favor of the Lord our God by turning from our iniquity and giving attention to Your truth" (Daniel 9:13). Not only will calamity fall upon our nation, but our allegiance will be revealed as well. Jesus told the Pharisees, "If God were your Father, you would love me, . . . Why can't you understand what I am saying? It's because you can't even hear me! For you are the children of your father the devil, and you love to do the evil things he does. He was a murderer from the beginning. He has always hated the truth, because there is no truth in him. Anyone who belongs to God listens gladly to the words of God. But you don't listen because you don't belong to God" (John 8:43-47 - NLT).

In one of my churches a couple came forward to join the church. Reading their contact information, I realized they were single and living together. I sat down with the couple while the congregation was singing and explained the biblical view of marriage. They agreed to counseling with me. Long story short, they came to know Jesus. I baptized them and then married them.

On another occasion, a young man came to me to see if I would marry him and his girlfriend. They wanted a Christian wedding. He said they were living together. Since they had family in town, I suggested they separate until the wedding. "Great idea," he said. Well, two weeks later, I received an email that he secured a liberal pastor to do the wedding.

The sexual revolution divulges whom our nation desires to follow, and is following because our nation upholds transgender, homosexual, and cohabitation lifestyles. In other words, we have become a godless nation out to please our fleshly desires. Except for marital sex, biblical truth tells us to abstain from sexual activity. God's judgement is upon us because most do not control their sexual appetites. Most don't know Truth!

NEVER NULLIFY THE GRACE OF GOD

"I do not nullify the grace of God, for if righteousness were through the law, then Christ died for no purpose"
(Galatians 2:21).

Nullify or in the Greek, "atheteo," means to "thwart the efficacy of anything, make void, to do away with, or disregard." Grace, God's undeserved favor, is throughout Scripture. From the beginning in Genesis, when Adam and Eve were removed from the Garden, they were clothed by God. When Moses led the Israelites out of Egypt, they repeatedly experienced God's grace by a pillar of cloud by day, and a pillar of fire by night (Exodus 13:20-22). From the parting of the Red Sea in order to escape Pharaoh's army, to God providing for them during their wilderness journey with quail and manna, God provided grace to the Israelites. There are numerous other examples in the Old Testament of God's favor.

In the New Testament the main theme of God's grace is around salvation. Individuals salvation is by God's grace alone. There is nothing one can do to earn salvation. No works, decision, or religion can bring someone into a relationship with Jesus.

Without grace everyone is bound for Hell. Religion and the law cannot produce righteousness in a person's life.

Christ's death, burial, and resurrection fulfilled the law. Jesus is alive and He is bringing all His elected saints into a relationship with Him by grace. Theologian Warren Wiersbe weighs in by saying, "the Law says DO! Grace says DONE!" Jesus on the cross said, "It is finished!" (John 19:30). His finished work was to provide grace, not the law or religion, for salvation. As the lesson's text states, if the law or religion was a means to salvation, then Christ died needlessly thus without purpose.

One must understand that everyone is dead in their sin (Ephesians 2:1). A dead person cannot bring himself back to life. Some believe that people are not completely dead when their spiritual heart stops beating, but they are just sick or they have enough breath in them to make a declaration for Christ. No, dead means dead! There is no ability to make a choice for Christ. John recorded Jesus statement about one's inability, "No one can come to Me unless the Father who sent Me draws him, and I will raise him up at the last day (6:44). Jesus states, "no one can." In other words, humankind has lost the ability to come to Jesus. The drawing by the Father is not a wooing, but a compelling by the Father. Draw, "helko" in the Greek, is the same word in James 2:6 when the rich will drag (helko) the poor into court. The translators of John 6:44 use the word "compel" to describe the Father's workings or drawing in a life.

The golden chain of salvation helps to understand the drawing of God by grace in salvation. Romans 8:29-30 describes this chain. Those whom are foreknown (known before the foundation of the world), they are predestined (chosen for salvation), those predestined are called (effective calling, not a wooing, a call that will compel a person to come), those called will be justified (a legal term with a one-time declaration of being not guilty before God), those justified will be glorified (made into the perfect image of God).

The dead person is regenerated through the Holy Spirit's calling of the person. That person's nature has been changed and now the person is spiritually alive. The law didn't do it nor religion, but the workings of God's grace through the resurrected Jesus did it.

If grace is nullified or done away with, every person on the planet has no hope; however, the resurrected Jesus makes us alive through His amazing grace. Newton was right in his hymn, "Amazing Grace" that God takes a wretched person (dead in sin), and saves or calls the person. They were lost but now they are found, and they were blind but now they see. All by grace (Ephesians 2:8-10). The amazing aspect of salvation is that the Lord now lives in a person's life that was dead in their sin. Leslie Fields poem, "Let the Stable Still Astonish," reveals why grace must never be nullified:

> "Straw-dirt floor, dull eyes, dusty flanks of donkeys, oxen; crumbling, crooked wall; No bed to carry that pain, and then the child, rag-wrapped, laid to cry in a trough. Who would have chosen this? Who would have said: "Yes, let the God of all the heavens and earth be born, in this place? Who but the same God- who stands in the darker, fowler rooms of our hearts and says, "Yes, let the God of Heaven and earth be born here in this place."

Our incurable, desperately wicked, deceitful, and dead hearts are where God finds a new home to reside. His Spirit lives within us to bring us to life for His glory. Yes, if grace were nullified, then we all would be living as zombies – bodies without regenerated souls.

Nation of the Truth

"You shall say to them, 'This is the nation that did not obey the voice of the Lord their God or accept correction; truth has perished and has been cut off from their mouth" (Jeremiah 7:28).

"These are the things which you should do: speak the truth to one another; judge with truth and judgment for peace in your gates" (Zechariah 8:16 NASB 1995).

"The Christian faith is not true because it works; it works because it is true. It is not true because we experience it; we experience it-deeply and gloriously – because it is true" (Oz Guinness).

From where does a nation glean its truth? Jeremiah's prophecy three thousand years ago is applicable today. Truth has perished, and it has been cut off from our country. Guinness is spot on in his assessments of truth.

"Faith is true "because it works" (pragmatism), because they feel it is true in their experience (subjectivism), ... it is true for them (relativism). ... All truth is God's truth and is true everywhere, for everyone under all conditions. ... truth does not yield to opinion, fashion, numbers, office, or sincerity – it is simply true ..."

Nation of the Truth

Our culture has replaced true-Truth with opinion, feelings, experience, and whoever yells the loudest. This is why many lawmakers listen to the loud static of a few people instead of the clarity of God's Truth. Decision makers have only allowed public outcry to sway their decision making, and they have dismissed any theological oversight of policy for our nation.

In America, one might say the Declaration of Independence is the source of truth; however, the Supreme Court can interpret an issue based on popular opinion rather than from original intent of the founding fathers. The glaring example is the Supreme Court's decision, (5-4), in June 2015. On that date, the approval of gay marriage based on the Constitution's statement of "Life, Liberty, and the pursuit of Happiness." What is missing from the Court's decision? The issue of morality. Where does one find the moral truth about marriage? Where is the historical tradition of marriage formulated? Historically, the tradition in the United States has been that marriage is between a man and woman. The arrangement for traditional marriage flows from the Bible (Genesis 2:24). Jesus reiterated the text in Matthew's gospel (19:5), and then the Apostle Paul elaborated on the Scripture in his letter to the Ephesians (5:31). Throughout America's history there have been homosexuals. Yes, the homosexual community is entitled to life, liberty, and the pursuit of happiness from our government. But not at the expense of centuries of marital biblical truth.

Today culturally, there is an under-current of Marxist ideology in our nation. These followers believe that capitalism is an evil, making this ideology unfair for the masses in America. However, capitalism has been the vehicle God has used for mankind to work and prosper to use his God given giftedness for His glory. Yes, we are to maintain a lifestyle that would allow for helping others, but it is not the government's role to dictate through higher taxes, how much of a person's taxes are to be given away to help others. Higher personal taxes will only stymie creativity, and the enthusiasm to work. Granted, even among Christians there is greed and a higher than necessary lifestyle, but the government is not to be the police force to correct this unfairness.

Initially, Black Lives Matter (BLM) on their website promoted the destruction of the nuclear family. Currently, it has been removed from their website. The family is the first institution God created, and it is the fabric of any nation. This Marxist group is trying to bully others into advocating their agenda to destroy the family unit which holds America together.

Educationally, the current movement is to indoctrinate students with the 1619 belief that this is when America began. True, it is when the first black individuals came onto this new land. However, the 1776 date is when America won its freedom from the British, in the Revolutionary War, to become an independent nation. In 1619, the British were still the ruling nation of the new-found land.

The Declaration of Independence states that we are "endowed by their Creator . . ." Many of the signers of the document held to a Christian belief around God. Zechariah is right that a nation needs to speak truth to each other and judge with truth, for peace to be in the land. If prosperity, security, and freedom are to be maintained in America, the nation must be a nation of the Truth, not truthiness – the fabrication of facts.

Since 1999, there is a monument atop Pikes Peak that shares the words of Katherine Lee Bates popular hymn, "America the Beautiful." Bates, a former teacher at Wellesley College, spent a summer teaching at a Colorado college in 1893. While traveling across the country, the poem, "America the Beautiful," was beginning to be conceptualized, and when visiting Pikes Peak her poem crystalized. The poem was first considered be America's patriotic song. The thirty-three-year-old teacher wrote the weighty lyric in her poem:

"America! America! God shed His grace on thee."

My question to our country is, is God withdrawing His grace from America?

What has been undermining our culture to erode our nation to the point of collapsing our economy, turning our heads toward atheism or godlessness, becoming a politically socialistic- progressive nation, and potentially into a sinkhole of governmental dictatorship? The answer is our country has rejected God and His Word as the focus texts states. This is why we must plead with God to send a tsunami of grace and truth once again upon America.

ONLY BY GRACE IS SOMEONE BORN AGAIN

> "And you were dead in the trespasses and sins in which you once walked . . . vv1-3; But God, being rich in mercy, because of the great love with which he loved us, even when we were dead in our trespasses, made us alive together with Christ – by **grace** you have been saved . . . vv4-7; For by **grace** you have been saved through faith. And this is not your own doing; it is the gift of God, not a result of works, so that no one may boast . . ." vv8-9 (Ephesians 2:1-9).

I stand amazed that so many Christians think they contributed to their salvation. Whether through a prayer, a decision, or works, many believe that they participated in their ability to be born again. Every religion in the world, expect for Christianity, holds to a belief system of works. However, even in the Christian community, their emphasis is around human responsibility or free will.

Sadly, many in the Christian faith hold to the fact that they, in a passive way, contributed to their salvation. No one believes that they can merit salvation by doing good deeds like knocking on doors. However, the element of free will creeps into the conversation of being born again. Most would say that one would have to choose to repent, then God will make them alive to Him or regenerated.

We must understand that free will is governed by what motivates us the most. Every day we make decisions based on our strongest motivations. After a meal, if I'm on a diet, do I have dessert or not? This weighs on our decision-making. Which is the strongest motivation, dieting or a favorite dessert? Our sinful, wicked heart's motivation is always toward what we want, and not God. Until our hearts are regenerated or we are born from above, our strongest motivation/inclination for God won't occur. Yes, we have free will, but our wills are not totally free until God becomes our strongest motivation.

Breaking the focus text down, we see the genesis of our having total free will. Total free will is the fact of having the ability to choose Jesus. The obvious fact one notices in the text is that all people are "dead in their trespasses and sins" (Ephesians 2:1). David stated this in Psalm 51, "Behold, I was brought forth in iniquity, and in sin did my mother conceive me." We all were born sinners.

Now a dead person spiritually cannot respond to God nor has the free will to do so. If you are dead, you are dead. Through original sin's consequences, we lost the ability to choose Christ. In essence, everyone is born as a 'zombie." Born alive physically, but dead spiritually. To repeat from a former chapter, John 6:44 states that we have lost the ability, or as Saint Augustine wrote, "we lost the liberty," to come to the Jesus. Again, everyone is dead spiritually as Paul stated.

Then Paul wrote, "but God!" not, "but me!" God makes a person alive in Christ. God's grace gives the gift of faith to believe and to repent of one's sins. Now our wills are free to be able to accept the effective call of God for salvation. The effective call of God means that I will come, and I will desire to come to Jesus in faith. Faith is not created, imagined, bought by someone, but it is given as a gift through God's grace. "Faith is the fruit of regeneration."

I've heard Christian leaders say to just reach up and take Jesus' hand. For example, let's say someone is in a boat, and he falls over and is drowning. Soon, a boat comes by and those on the boat yell, "reach for the life preserver!" Those who believe that a person is **not** totally dead spiritually believe the person can reach out for the lifesaving device. It is the person's will that rescues his life.

A totally opposite example of the illustration, the boat comes up besides the drowning man and a person on the boat pulls him out and starts CPR on the individual to bring him back to life. This is what God does. He comes to a spiritually dead person with grace. God's grace gifts the person with faith so he can believe. It's not me holding on to God, but God gripping me.

Remember October 13, 2010 in Chile where 33 men were trapped some 2200 feet in the earth's belly. They were there for 69 days in 95-degree heat. These men could not save themselves. The United States and several other countries rallied around the tragedy. Through their funds and ingenuity, they designed a capsule that was lowered into the area of the 33 men. One by one these men were rescued. Likewise, we cannot save ourselves; we need someone outside of ourselves to help us for our salvation.

Paul wrote that the Ephesians were chosen before the foundation of the world. Jesus stated, recorded in John 15:16, "You did not choose Me, but I chose you . . ." God in His divine sovereignty will rescue those whom He has chosen before the foundation of the world (Ephesians 1:4). No one knows who the elect are, so we teach and preach, "whosoever will." Whosoever will by the grace of God, through faith, confesses Jesus will be saved (Romans 10:10-13). The born-again person believes in the death, burial, and resurrection of Jesus according to the Scriptures (I Corinthians 15:1-4). Their confession will lead them to display spiritual fruit of repentance in their lives through their character and service. The born-again person has a life change that will be recognized by others.

The person of faith, given by God's grace, who has a changed will, will come to Jesus, and he will be rescued from being dead spiritually, to be alive in Jesus. Thus, he will only want to boast in Jesus because of the grace given to him to have faith to believe. The boast is not to look at what I've done but observe what Christ has done in and through me. We boast in our salvation that is through the five solas: Scripture alone, Christ alone, grace alone, faith alone, and for the glory of God alone.

Overcomers for the Truth

"These things I have spoken to you, that in Me you may have peace. In the world you will have tribulation; but take courage, I have overcome the world" (John 16:33).

Knowing the condition of the world, and especially the United States, some would desire to throw up their hands and exclaim, "What is the use? It is hopeless!" Watching the erosion of America makes one's heart break. People have abandoned the Truth for a lie. The Apostle John's text could be a news headline, "Tribulation in the World!" Without a doubt, there is tribulation in our world. Many attempt to escape the tribulation by searching for peace through pills, drugs, sex, work, and material possessions. However, the Christian is called to be an overcomer. Putting on the Scriptural armor (Ephesians 6:10f) will allow one to overcome the lie with the truth.

First and foremost, one must put on Jesus Christ (Romans 13:14). John is clear when he writes, "For everyone who has been born of God overcomes the world. And this is the victory that has overcome the world—our faith" (I John 5:4-5). It is the faith that believes that Jesus is the way, the truth, and the life, and except through Him no one comes to the Father (John 14:6). The Apostle Paul exhorts the faithful to put on the helmet of salvation (Ephesians 6:17). In addition, the faithful follower of Jesus believes that Jesus is God (I John 5:20).

Second, salvation in Jesus promises that the third Person of the Trinity will live within the believer. "Little children, you are from God and have overcome them, for He who is in you is greater than he who is in the world" (I John 4:4). That is to say, that the Holy Spirit is more powerful and wiser than Satan. The Holy Spirit, not Satan, teaches truth. "When the Spirit of truth comes, he will guide you into all the truth... (John 16:13).

Third, the believer puts on the belt of truth (Ephesians 6:14). Other parts of the armor are tethered to the belt of truth. One of those joined to the belt of truth is the fourth piece of armor, the sword (Ephesians 6:17b), which is the Word of God (Hebrews 4:12). This book, the Bible, is where truth is located for the believer and the world. Again, John writes, ". . . I write to you, young men, because you are strong, and the word of God abides in you, and you have overcome the evil one" (I John 2:14). The other piece of armor fastened to the belt of truth as cited in Ephesians 6 is the breast plate of righteousness (v16b), which protects the heart. Additional armor not attached to the belt of truth includes the gospel of peace to cover the feet for firm footing (v15), and the shield of faith to quench the fiery darts of lies (v16).

On the battlefield of lies, the soldier of faith is exhorted not to fight underhandly. In other words, "Do not be overcome by evil, but overcome evil with good" (Romans 12:21). The "armor of light" (Romans 13:12) has been put on, and now the warrior of the Truth will walk in holiness as he is protected from the devil's temptations of fleshly desires and lies (Romans 13:13-14).

Dressed in armor for battle, the truth warrior now can be salt and light in the world (Matthew 5:13-16). The battlefield of lies is where one fights for truth. Even if heartache, pain, and maybe even death, come on the battlefield, will the church be faithful? Throughout church history, the church flourishes when the blood of her warriors becomes the seeds to grow the truth. The faithful overcomers will be courageous giving hope to America. For even though there is great tribulation, the warrior has great bravery because he knows the Lord has overcome the world.

In overcoming the world, the Lord has given "peace with God" (Romans 5:1) to all who believe on His Name and works. This is huge! Now there is "no condemnation for those who are in Christ Jesus" (Romans 8:1). In other words, Hell has been removed from our birth resume. For all have sinned and the wage of sin is death (Romans 3:23, 6:23). In death without Christ one is bound for Hell. But having the "peace with God" guarantees us Heaven.

The other good news of Jesus overcoming the world is we have the "peace of God" (Philippians 4:7). This peace, as Paul describes, "will guard our hearts and minds." Instead of being discouraged and overcome by life circumstances, the believer knows that the Word of God and the Holy Spirit will bring protection to his heart and mind (Romans 8). Now, as overcomers, you will know the truth and the truth will indeed set you free.

PRESENCE OF GOD AT THE THRONE OF GRACE

"Let us then with confidence draw near to the throne of grace,
that we may receive mercy and fine grace
to help in time of need" (Hebrews 4:16).

This verse pictures a contrast between what the Old Testament teaches about approaching God, and how the New Testament instructs about approaching God. In the Old Testament, the Levitical high priest made a sacrifice for the sins of Israel on the Day of Atonement. After he went through a purification ritual, the high priest entered the Holy of Holies or Holy Place in the Tabernacle, and offered a blood atonement from a bull or goat. The high priest put blood on the Mercy Seat of the Ark of the Covenant (which represented the presence of God) as an atonement for the sins of his people. Next, there was a blessing over a scapegoat and then it was released into the wilderness symbolizing all the sins of the nation would be forgiven (Leviticus 16-17, Hebrews 9-10).

In the New Testament, a Christian seeking comfort has direct access to the throne which the Hebrew writer calls the throne of grace. The doctrine is called the 'Priesthood of the Believer.' This means Christians believe, like a priest, that they have direct access to the High Priest – Jesus. No one must go through a priest, clergy, or Pope to have admittance to Jesus. It does not mean that the Christian can interpret the Bible anyway he chooses. He simply has access to God.

In the book of Esther, the common practice where kings were unapproachable is explained. Queen Esther put her life on the line by going to King Ahasuerus without an invitation on behalf of the Jewish nation (5:1-2).

Totally opposite, no matter how sinful, disobedient, or needy the believer is, they are welcomed at the throne of grace without an invitation or a fear of being killed like Esther.

"Let us draw near" is a gracious invitation to come to our High Priest without fear. This means we can approach His throne of grace with "confidence" or boldness knowing He cares for us. On that dark day on Calvary's Hill, Jesus shed His blood as a substitution for our sins. As the earth quaked, the Temple curtain that separated the people from the high Priest was torn in half. This signified that all are welcome to come into the Holy Place (Matthew 27:51). To draw near is to come facing forward to embrace. In the Greek present tense, it is a continually coming forward to Jesus in prayer, worship, and devotion; not just on a certain day like the Day of Atonement.

The Christian draws near with "confidence." It literally means all speech or speaking all things, which conveys the idea of freedom to say whatever is on the heart or mind. The person is assured that he will be heard, not silenced. Again, unlike Queen Esther, the believer can come into the presence of Jesus without fear. He can express whatever is on his heart with boldness or with confidence at the throne of grace.

The "throne of grace" to the unbeliever is a throne of judgement. But to the saint it is a throne of grace where help is asked for, burdens are expressed, and needs shared. The High Priest, Jesus, welcomes our approach to His throne. A throne is a lofty, authoritarian place. Grace speaks of kindness and understanding. Jesus blends these characteristics together to shower upon the seeker undeserved favor. Again, it was the unapproachable throne for the Israelites, except for their high Priest.

"Grace is that which brings joy. The joy comes through the freeness in a gift or favor. It is the free, spontaneous, absolute, loving kindness of God toward men" (Vincent, Word Studies in NT, vol. 4, page 109). Preacher of yesteryear, Dr. Donald Barnhouse writes, "love that stoops is grace."

Mercy is not getting what we deserve; whereas, grace is getting what we do not deserve. Mercy, Wuest writes, is "God's kindness and goodwill toward the miserable and afflicted; joined with a desire to relieve them." When one cries out with confidence at the throne of grace, the person will receive help. As I stated in an earlier chapter, this is well-timed help. That is to say, the help comes in God's time not our timetable. In other words, grace that comes to us is "well- timed by God" (John Piper).

Crying out at the throne of grace, one enters into worship-based prayer." Daniel Henderson, in his book, *21 Days of Transforming Prayer*, writes, "Worship-based prayer" seeks the face of God before the hand of God. God's face is the essence of who He is. God's hand is the blessing of what He does. God's face represents His person and presence. God's hand expresses His provision for needs in our lives. I learned that if all we ever do is seek God's hand, we miss His face; but if we seek His face, He will be glad to open His hand and satisfy the deepest desires of our hearts." We come with one motivation in mind, that whatever we ask will bring glory to His name. The Psalmist writes, "Not unto us LORD, not unto us, but to your name give glory" (115:1).

To come with confidence to the throne of grace is to approach His throne to see and hear from God first. Then we ask for His help in our time of need. Praise the Lord that this verse is like a welcome mat at a front door. Hebrews 4:16 reminds the reader that God's presence is always welcoming and comforting.

PRACTICE OF THE TRUTH

"If we say that we have fellowship with Him and *yet* walk in the
darkness, we lie and do not practice the truth;"
(I John 1:8).

"But he who practices the truth comes to the Light, so that
his deeds may be manifested as having been wrought in God"
(John 3:21)

"The one who says, "I have come to know Him," and does not
keep His commandments, is a liar, and the
truth is not in him;" (I John 2:4).

When one hears the word practice, one often associates the word with sports. To practice is to do something repeatedly until that thing becomes second nature to the person. My favorite play in all of sports is the double play in baseball. It is a play that requires accuracy of a throw to second, which requires a gymnastic type move around the second base bag to make a throw to first, where the first baseman usually stretches out to catch the ball. To perform this play at the professional level, many hours of practice are required to make the double play look effortless.

In the theological arena, to practice truth is similar to the meaning in sports. One has to repeat the truth so that it will become second nature to him. When a person is born again and regenerated, godly-life practices can develop to replace the old habits of life. For example, instead of watching sports on a Sunday morning, the convert is in church. Athletes have an inner desire to please their coach and fans. Likewise, the new Christian's desire is to glorify the Lord. As the new lifestyle develops over time, church going eventually becomes an involuntary action.

To react automatically to a play, a baseball player is taught to think through the game situation prior to the ball possibly being hit to him. John, in his gospel, states if one practices the truth, he spontaneously desires to glorify Jesus, the Light (John 3:21). The aim is to show others the new life deeds that come from God. Polar opposite is John's statement in his first letter. One cannot say "I have fellowship with God" and live in lies. That person does not practice truth. Secondly, one who says, "I know Him," but fails to keep God's commandments is a liar. These never come or desire to come to the Light. For example, in politics, I hear lawmakers say they love God and they say, "God bless America." How can God bless our nation when the lawmakers stand for lifestyles that are in opposition to the Word of God. Like abortion, transgenderism, open borders, climate control, and gay marriage. Do these lawmakers really know God and the Lord Jesus Christ?

You see, practicing truth is desiring to keep God's commandments. This occurs through the sanctification process of a believer where the Holy Spirit is working in the believer's life in concert with the Word of God. Then the believer will eventually love others and keep God's law instinctively.

Practicing truth gives the believer an advantage of knowing how to confront pseudo-truths. A barrage of lies is released daily through the news medias, political arenas, Hollywood, and even the church. The Bible is clear that numerous false teachers will be in the world. In order to distinguish between what is true and what is false, the Christian must be discerning, wise, and knowledgeable of Scripture.

Most play the mind game of the "what ifs" in life. They look to the future anticipating something bad happening to them. Some people live in this realm thinking that the sky is going to fall at any time. Consequently, the people who live like this remain in constant turmoil, which can lead to depression, discouragement, and dissatisfaction.

On the other hand, the "even ifs" have truth that turns the negative thinking into a positive outlook because one places the problem under the microscope of Scripture – truth. Listen to Habakkuk 3:17-19, *"Even if* the fig tree does not bloom and the vines have no grapes, *even if* the olive tree fails to produce and the fields yield no food, *even if* the sheep pen is empty and the stalls have no cattle even then, I will be happy with the LORD. I will truly find joy in God, who saves me."

Many learn that they need to place their heads each night on the "sovereign pillow" of God. By practicing truth before others, they will see how effortlessly you are handling your life circumstances. This life-play of trusting God and practicing truth far exceeds the beauty of baseball's double play.

Qualified to Preach the Grace of God

"For this reason, I, Paul, the prisoner of Christ Jesus for the sake of you Gentiles- if indeed you have heard of the stewardship of God's **grace** which was given to me for you; vv1-2. 7-8: of which I was made a minister, according to the gift of God's **grace** which was given to me according to the working of His power. To me, the very least of all saints, this **grace** was given, to preach to the Gentiles the unfathomable riches of Christ" (Ephesians 3:1-8).

To teach or preach "the unfathomable, or unsearchable riches of Christ," a person (male) needs a degree from a seminary. Yes, there are some who preach without a seminary degree, but most have one. Whether someone has a degree or not, the main qualifier to preach is God's grace. By God's grace, Paul was called to preach to the Gentiles.

I addressed preaching ministry only to males. The primary reason is the Bible says so. The word "elder" is always masculine and plural. In 1Peter 5:1-4, one finds three words to describe the leadership of the church: Presbuteros (elder), poimen (shepherd), and episkopeo (overseer or guardian). According to Peter, the elder is to exercise oversight as a shepherd, not heavy handed, but with delight, as an example to the flock. In order to equip the saints for the work of ministry, he ministers as Peter describes. God, as Ephesians 4 explains, appoints men to be shepherds and teachers.

When I was called to preach, I was at a crossroad. The athletic director of my high school offered me the varsity basketball coaching position. This was my dream job. Since playing in high school and college, I always wanted to coach basketball. I hoped my future career would be a college coach. After discussing the opportunity with my wife, and through much prayer, I opted to accept the call to preach. After a semester at a very liberal seminary, I withdrew and returned to teaching and coaching. Three years later, after a revival, I told my wife that I needed to go back to seminary. Returning to the same seminary, which had become less liberal, I was able to complete my degree. While completing my degree, I pastored a church in my hometown and commuted to seminary twice a week. The Lord sent a family to my first church where the husband was a graduate of a very conservative seminary. He gave me his books which kept me on a conservative learning track. Until my health forced me to retire, my preaching journey lasted forty-three years. I believe, like Paul, God had an effective call upon my life to preach.

Paul was appointed, before the foundation of the world (Galatians 1:15), by the management of God's grace to be an Apostle to preach to the Gentiles. Holding this position, Paul was appointed to be a steward or manager of God's grace in declaring the unsearchable riches of Christ Jesus.

Until Acts 9, Paul, then Saul, had no plans in being a voice for the Lord. In fact, he was an antagonist or enemy of the Christian church. But under God's sovereign plan of grace, Paul fulfilled the design to accomplish God's plan for him to preach to the Gentiles. As the focus text highlights, grace was a gift given to Paul to preach to the Gentiles. Now salvation was offered through Paul to both the Jewish and Gentile communities.

One preacher told a young man who was considering going into the preaching ministry, "if you can do anything else, go do it." The young man was confused by the preacher's statement. After digesting the comment, the young man asked the preacher what he meant. He said, "When you cannot do anything else, you know you have the call of God upon your life to preach."

Another young man was going into the ministry. He asked for advice from a more seasoned pastor if he should accept the call to ministry. The pastor said, "If money, fame, criticism, and hard work are no obstacles to you, then go and preach."

A young preacher came to me for advice concerning the pastoral ministry. I said, "There are four areas you must keep before you at all times: Prayer, Purity, Proclamation of the gospel by exegesis preaching, and Paraclete (Holy Spirit) ministry – showing the nine-character Holy Spirit fruit from Galatians 5:22-23: love, joy, peace, patience, kindness, goodness, faithfulness, gentleness, self-control to the flock."

Like Paul, the Holy Spirit gives all His followers grace to achieve ministry purposes for the glory of God. Whether you minister to children, teenagers, or adults in some capacity, your ministry is a gift of grace to you for the building up of the body of Christ – His church. Ministry gifts are appointed by the Holy Spirit (I Corinthians 12:11). The Lord qualifies you by giving you grace to perform the task he has for you.

The bottom line is this, like Paul, what qualifies us to minister in the name of Jesus is the grace of God. Many have gone into various ministries on their own strength. Most become frustrated and they slowly die out from that ministry. I believe when one is truly called to a ministry, he or she will fulfill that ministry through the grace of God.

QUANDARY AROUND THE TRUTH

"Jesus Christ: a liar, a lunatic, or Lord?"
- C.S. Lewis, *Mere Christianity*

"Now, therefore, fear the Lord and serve Him in sincerity and truth; and put away the gods which your fathers served beyond the River and in Egypt, and serve the Lord"
(Joshua 24:14).

C.S. Lewis' book the *The Silver Chair* is about Jill who is lost and thirsty in a strange land. She finds a brook, but she sees Aslan, the Lion (a symbol of Christ) lying beside the brook. Aslan growls and tells her she may come and drink.

"May I...could I...would you mind going away while I drink," said Jill.

The Lion answered with a look and very low growl and Jill gazed at its motionless bulk, she realized that she might as well have asked the whole mountain to move aside for her convenience. The delicious rippling noise of the stream was driving her nearly frantic.

"Do you promise not to do anything to me if I do come?"

Quandary Around the Truth

"I promise," said the Lion.

Jill was thirsty now that, without noticing it, she had come a step closer.

"Do you eat girls?" she said.

"I have swallowed up girls and boys, women and men, kings and emperors, cities and towns," said the Lion.

"I dare not come and drink," said Jill

"Then you will die of thirst," said the Lion.

"Oh, dear," said Jill coming a step closer. "I suppose I must go and look for another stream then."

"There is no other stream," said the Lion.

People are looking for a stream to satisfy their worldly thirst. They drink from the wells of the earth and leave with their thirst unquenched. Like the lady at the well (John 4:13-14). Jesus said, if you drink from Jacob's well you will always be thirsty. In verse 13, "drink" is in the present tense which means to continually to drink. Jesus continued, but if you drink from Me, you will never thirst again. Now in verse 14, the word "drink" is in the aorist tense which means a one-time action with ongoing results. The lady at the well had five husbands and was presently living with another man. Jesus is teaching her that through Him she will find peace in her life. In fact, Jesus gave her a wonderful promise – "The water that I will give him will become in him a spring of water welling up to eternal life." Likewise, Aslan is telling Jill that only this stream will satisfy her thirst. This stream can only come through Jesus Christ.

The Lewis reference at the beginning of this chapter from *Mere Christianity* shows the complexity of Truth, which is that most people do not see Jesus as Lord. Their idols have been placed before the face of God. Is Jesus a liar - teaching lies to manipulate or maneuver people into His web of thinking and living? Most folks have positioned reason over revelation. Is Jesus a lunatic with crazy, wild, and unreasonable teachings like the cult leader Jim Jones who had his followers "drink the Kool-Aid," killing 918 followers in 1978?

The quandary or complexity can be resolved by following the Joshua focus text – "Fear the Lord, serve Him in integrity and truth." But the challenge comes in putting away the gods one follows. Only then will the first part of the text come to fruition. In Lewis' *The Silver Chair* he wrote, "There is no other stream." Until one realizes that there is nothing in the world that will douse a thirsty soul except Jesus, people will continue to run to the streams of their god - work, recreation, sports, sex, alcohol, drugs, and food to quench the inner desire for peace of the soul and life. Sadly, individuals have allowed science to replace biblical teaching. Science has become the god of the land, and biblical teaching is regarded as outdated or worse, as lunacy. How about the god of government? Will socialism, where the citizenry depends on the government to provide for their needs bring peace of life? All the gods one serves are liars, except Creator God. The real lunatics of life are the people who chase after these gods. Observe the number incarcerated, the many in rehab or recovery facilities, the statistics for divorces, and the high rate of suicides. One has to ask, who is really the liar and lunatic?

Jesus gives the promise, "If anyone is thirsty, let him come to Me and drink, He who believes in Me, as the Scripture said, 'From his innermost being will flow rivers of living water'" (John 7: 37-38). The living water is Jesus flowing through you. These waters contain love, joy, peace, patience, kindness, goodness, faithfulness, gentleness, self-control (Galatians 5:22). The quandary or complexity of truth is resolved in Jesus. Jesus will only be Lord when you have been born again to see and enter the kingdom of God (John 3:3,5).

Won't you come kneel beside and drink from the stream of life – Jesus?

RICHES OF GOD'S GRACE

"In Him we have redemption through His blood, the forgiveness
of our trespasses, according to the riches of His grace..."
(Ephesians 1:7).

Ephesians 1: 1-14 is one long Greek sentence filled with promises of hope. In verse 4, we learn that we were chosen, elected, or *selected* before the foundation of the world (2 Timothy 1:9, *before time began*). Then in verse 7, we read that Jesus *saved* us. Finally, in verse 13, our salvation is *sealed* by the Holy Spirit.

Hope in the Bible means "certainty" or a "guarantee." It doesn't mean "wishful thinking" - like I wish it would not rain on my outing. Salvation for the believer in Jesus was manifested through the love-work of God before time began. The elect, those whose lives have been regenerated, born again, will come to Jesus when they are effectively called. The Reformed view holds to the fact that we don't wish some will come to Christ, we are filled with hope or certainty that many will come to Him. Jesus told His disciples in John 4:35, "Do you not say there are four months then comes the harvest? Look, I tell you, lift up your eyes, and see that the fields are white for harvest." In other words, Jesus, who is sovereign, says, I know many are ready to come into the kingdom. In fact, the Apostle Paul stated, "Therefore, I endure everything for the sake of the elect, that they also may obtain the salvation that is in Christ Jesus with eternal glory" (2 Timothy 2:10).

Verse 7 is the highwater mark of the fourteen verses. "In Him," Jesus, paid a price to set the sinner free from the weight of being a slave to a sinful life. His blood was the atonement of sins and turned the wrath of God away from all who believe (propitiation). Jesus did for sinful humanity what they could not do for themselves. The Bible states, that Jesus is our substitute. This makes His cross bearing a substitutionary atonement for the elect. All who believe are the elect of God.

The price paid for our salvation, the blood of Jesus, means that we are forgiven. Every sin committed, past, present, and in the future has been paid for. This doesn't free us to sin. Even though we are saved, we must still realize that sin has consequences; but Hell has been erased from our life's history.

The believer's forgiveness carries with it a responsibility. For example, every believer has to forgive others. A sure sign of one's election is the willingness to forgive others. Jesus made it clear, if one cannot forgive, then his sins will not be forgiven (Matthew 6:14-15). An unforgiving spirit can create a 'root of bitterness' (Hebrews 12:15) in the unforgiving person.

The redemption for our salvation and the forgiveness we receive, both flow from the *riches of God's grace*. Riches is the abundance that God lavishes on His elect. The undeserved favor that flows from heaven never ceases.

My wife and I spent time in Niagara Falls. Wearing rain gear, we went under the falls on the Maid of the Mist. We didn't realize 3,160 tons of water flows over Niagara Falls every second which accounts for 75,750 gallons of water per second. Well, the flow rate of grace from heaven exceeds Niagara Falls water rate. John, in his prologue, writes in verse 16, that through the fulness of Christ we receive "grace upon grace." This is abundance, overflowing, an untold amount of grace-wealth being lavished upon us.

Elaborating on John Newton's "Amazing Grace," we once were spiritually lost but grace found us, and once we were spiritual blind but now we have grace-eyes to see the truth about life now and forever. The unbeliever is a soul wandering in the desert. He builds his life on a foundation of sand. He longs for an oasis of refreshment to come into his life. Jesus finds this wandering soul and places him the narrow path of righteousness. Jesus builds this man's life on a foundation of the Rock. And Jesus becomes his spring of eternal refreshment. This is amazing grace!

A blind person whose eyes are renewed, sees the color of the things he touched and smelled. Similarly, when the spiritually blind person finally sees, he sees the horribleness of his sin and the holiness of the God who opened his eyes. He observes the dirty roads of life he was walking. These were leading him to the dead ends of life. Like the lost soul, now found, he sees the delightful narrow path of righteousness. He now travels on this path that leads him to an abundant life of joy and peace. This too is amazing grace!

From our salvation to our daily activities, grace comes upon us. The unbeliever or pagan does not understand or acknowledge this. But everything we possess (mind, talents, material things, Godly relationships and more) comes from the grace filled hands of God. Again, David's prayer as recorded in I Chronicles 29:12a was this, "Both riches and honor come from you, and you rule over all."

What hope (certainty, guarantee) we have knowing that our Good Shepherd will provide all the grace we will ever need in our lifetime. He is "rich" in grace to take care of His children. And, yes, even though they don't acknowledge God's grace, the pagans of this world enjoy His common grace (Matthew 5:45) that they receive daily.

Rest well my friends knowing that you can sleep on the pillow of God's rich grace that He lavishes on you without cost.

Reconstruction of the Truth

"For they exchanged the truth of God for a lie and worshiped
and served the creature rather than the Creator,
who is blessed forever. Amen" (Romans 1:25).

"If everything is endlessly open to question and change,
then everything is permitted, nothing is forbidden, and literally
nothing is unthinkable." Os Guinness, *Time for Truth:* ….

Change is in the air in America. The revolution is philosophical, theological, and political. This new era of thought is not for the betterment of Americans. A reconstructionist in the cultural is one on the far-left in the three areas mentioned. Philosophically, humankind is the center of thought. Theologically, the Bible is outdated, and God is basically dead. There is more support for the Islamic faith than for the Christian faith in America. Politically, capitalism is evil, and the government is the god of the land. Guinness is spot-on, the flood gates have been thrust open to a "whatever." Whatever the human sinful mind can imagine could become a reality. Isaiah 1:4, "Ah, sinful nation, a people laden with iniquity, offspring of evildoers, children who deal corruptly! They have forsaken the LORD, they have despised the Holy One of Israel, they are utterly estranged."

The reconstructionist scheme didn't occur overnight. Its proponents worked below the water to create a revolution in America. Their strategy reminded me of the construction of the Brooklyn Bridge. In the late 1800's, the Brooklyn Bridge in New York City was under construction. This miracle bridge took seventeen years to build. Roebling, the overseeing engineer, of the bridge was criticized for not building the bridge faster. For four years the community could not see construction above the water. Roebling's response was epic: "Men have risked their lives building a strong foundation below the waterline. If this important work was not done below the waterline what was built above the waterline would not stand the test of time." Christianity is built on the foundation of the death, burial, and resurrection of Jesus Christ. His Word, the Bible, is part of this foundation. Consequently, nothing will be able to destroy the work of Christ. Even the work of these revolutionaries has been below the waterline for decades. The election of a far-left, progressive politician was the first real evidence that change was in the air. However, is the reconstructionism's foundation below the waterline so secure, that their ideologies will stand the test of time? It is only if Jesus uses them to bring judgement on America. John Calvin wrote, "When God wants to judge a nation, He gives them wicked rulers." The evil leader is the reconstructionist of the truth. Their lies are touted as truth. Behind their pseudo-truth is for them to have power and control. The entire climate change idea or "Green New Deal" ideology, is designed to control the American citizen. However, we should not be surprised. The Apostle Paul writes young Timothy, "But understand this, that in the last days there will come times of difficulty. For people will be lovers of self, lovers of money, proud, arrogant, abusive, disobedient to their parents, ungrateful, unholy, heartless, unappeasable, slanderous, without self-control, brutal, not loving good, treacherous, reckless, swollen with conceit, lovers of pleasure rather than lovers of God, having the appearance of godliness, but denying its power" (II Timothy 3:1-5). These may be the last days before Christ returns, or these may be the last days of America.

Francis Frangipane, in his book, *Holiness of Truth and the Presence of God*, writes, "Sin wears a cloak of deception. The pure in heart are no longer deceived by sin; but see themselves as sinners saved by grace. Hypocrisy (play acting) is no longer on stage. Truth is knowing God's heart as it was reveled in Christ, and it is knowing our own hearts in the light of God's grace." Modernization is flourishing, because God is no longer in the equation of a reconstructionist.

This ideologue advocate attempts to achieve something originating from their flesh, not from God. As the Apostle Paul wrote in the focus text, "For they exchanged the truth of God for a lie, . . ." When one is born again or regenerated, he sees the lies because he knows the truth. The unregenerate only sees through eyes of the flesh. Consequently, anything bizarre may happen.

Guinness is totally correct in saying, "literally nothing is unthinkable." We have seen the "unthinkable" at our southern border when people, twelve million to date, enter illegally, and then receive government support and, the right to vote. "Unthinkable" is the rawness of some far-left politician who promoted verbally attacking Republicans, in restaurants and other public places. In a child's first four years of life, some parents' call their children "Theybies." They do this so the child can decide what gender he desires to be - This is "unthinkable." "Unthinkable" is the killing of babies, especially ones who have been birthed. To date approximately, 64 million babies have been sacrificed on the altar of convenience.

The designers of pseudo-truth, who have operated under the waterline, have been churches, universities, Hollywood, and liberal politicians. What these institutions and individuals have done is to rework truth to exclude God – the true-Truth. Without the triune God, human imagination is god, and it will construct the "unthinkable." The "unthinkable" has reconstructed truth; they have exchanged the truth of God for a lie.

SUFFICIENCY OF GOD'S GRACE

> "Three times I pleaded with the Lord about this, that it should leave me. But He said to me, "My grace is sufficient for you, for my power is perfect in weakness" Therefore I will boast all the more gladly of my weaknesses, so that the power of Christ may rest upon me (2 Corinthians 12:8-9).

I heard a preacher state that we are either in a storm, coming out of a storm, or about to enter into a storm. The Apostle Paul was "pleading" with the Lord to have his storm come to an end. But Jesus said, "NO!" Have you ever received that answer from the Lord? I have.

In my forty-three years of ministry, I was plagued with health problems; especially heart related issues. In my first church I burned out. I was going to seminary twice a week and overseeing a young church. After graduating, I stood in the pulpit, looked out into the eyes of the congregation, and cried out, "I can't do this anymore!" I closed my Bible and walked out. In God's sovereign love, the deacons rallied behind me. After going through a ten-week recovery period, I was back overseeing the church.

After six-years of service at my first church, I left to accept a call from a church in the foothills of North Carolina. Here I had my first heart issue. My wife took me to a Charlotte hospital for a heart catherization.

I had to stay overnight, so my wife went back home which was an hour and half away. Upon returning home around four p.m., she received a call from our hometown. The person said, "This is Hill and Wood Funeral Home, where should we take the body." My wife's scream drowned out the laughter on the other end. Not knowing I was in the hospital; our prankster friend was calling to see how we were doing. It took him a while to calm my wife down and for him to apologize.

After three years in this church, the Lord called us to the capital of North Carolina. We served there for fourteen years. But in my third year of service, I had two heart attacks. One on a Friday, and the second on Saturday. The family was called in by the doctor who thought I wasn't going to make it. By God's grace I recovered. At that point, I was on heart medications and I visited a cardiologist regularly. This was quite a change for a forty-four-year-old, who had to make major life alterations. Not only did my heart fail me, but my eyes as well. Both of my retinas detached and they were reattached over a two-year period.

My final stop before I retired was back in my hometown where I served at the church I grew up in – First Baptist Church, Park Street. I continued to be hospitalized for heart issues. Plus, I had a procedure to draw debris out of my left eye. In addition, I had abdominal surgeries.

When I retired at sixty-four, I entered into the Transitional Pastor Ministry (TPM). This is where you serve a church for a year or two to help a church recover and find a new pastor. My first TPM was a two-year ministry where I experienced server bowel issues and heart related problems.

My second TPM was a year. During that time, I spent twenty-five days in the hospital with pancreatitis. Following my hospital stay, I had to be on a feeding tube for six months. Preaching with a tube in my nose was not a pleasant experience.

The third TPM was also a year and believe it or not, no real issues with my health occurred.

Sufficiency of God's Grace

Coming down the home stretch, I would be forced to stop ministry. This final TPM lasted four years. During my time with this church, I had a twisted colon emergency surgery. The result of this surgery left me with abdominal hernias. I had hernia surgery six months later. After the surgery, I had a heart event. I was diagnosed with congestive heart failure. A pacemaker was placed in my heart, and my ejection fraction rate was only thirty-five percent. Eighteen months later it dropped to twenty-two percent. My energy had fallen off dramatically. At seventy-three years old, I had to stop TPM. Throughout my years of ministry, I prayed that my health would improve. Like Paul, the answer was always "no," thus I had to maintain this thorn in my life. Without a doubt, my health problems allowed the power of Christ to work through me. Plus, it was a witness to the churches I served of the sufficiency of God's grace. The people saw me trust the Lord through my aliments, thus they believed they could do the same.

Many Sunday mornings I was exhausted, but the power of the Holy Spirit reenergized me to preach on those Sunday's. My son saw this firsthand. Because I was exhausted, my son drove me to preach a revival. My son helped me into the sanctuary. He said when I went up to preach it was like a light switch was turned on. No one would have known I was struggling with overtiredness.

Grace could be defined as **G**od **R**eaching **A**cross **C**hasms of life to **E**nergize. This is what Paul stated, he received power in his weakness. Thus, he boasted about his weaknesses because he gave witness that God was in control.

Not only is Jesus sovereign over our lives but He is sufficient as well. His sufficiency always gives enough of what we need, so we can navigate the storms of life. Grace is the rudder to guide us safely through the storm to shores of safety and peace.

I found in the 1917 *Eternal Praise* hymnal, a 1918 hymn, titled "His Grace is Sufficient for Me." The chorus reads: "At home or aboard, on this land or sea, God's wonderful grace is sufficient for me; I'm finding it true that wherever I may be, His grace is sufficient for me..."

In your tribulations and sufferings, may you trust God to navigate you through your storms. Yes, you might pray for healing or for the situation to end, but like Paul and me, God might say, "no." If this is the case, watch how God's grace will energize you to do what He desires for you to accomplish for His glory. God works best through our weaknesses, not our strengths.

SUFFERING FOR THE TRUTH

"Blessed are those who have been persecuted for the sake of righteousness, for theirs is the kingdom of heaven. Blessed are you when *people* insult you and persecute you, and falsely say all kinds of evil against you because of Me. Rejoice and be glad, for your reward in heaven is great; for in the same way they persecuted the prophets who were before you"
(Matt. 5:10-12).

"For we can do nothing against the truth, but *only* for the truth"
(II Corinthians 13:8).

"The blood of the martyrs is the seed of the church." Tertullian

In the Scriptures suffering is multidimensional. The Apostle Paul writes, "We are afflicted in every way, but not crushed; perplexed, but not driven to despair; persecuted, but not forsaken; struck down, but not destroyed" (II Corinthians 4:8-9). Probably, each reader, whether Christian or not, can describe a season of suffering. People's suffering is multi-colored. Some suffer from illnesses, financial difficulties, death of loved ones, broken marriages or families, and you can add your personal tribulation. But what about suffering for the truth? Nineteenth century Anglican bishop of Liverpool, J.C. Ryle writes, "True Christianity will cost a man the favor of the world. He must be content to be thought ill of by man if he pleases God. He must count it no strange thing to be mocked, ridiculed, slandered, persecuted, and even hated." It was the same with Peter and John before the Council in Acts 4:12, when they stated, "And there is salvation in no one else, for there is no other name under heaven given among men by which we must be saved." John 14:6 is probably the most hated text in Scripture. Jesus said, "I am the way, the truth, and the life, no one can come to the Father except through Me." Peter reiterated what he learned from Jesus' teachings. In the Acts 4 event, the Council reprimanded them, and then let Peter and John go.

Throughout church history martyrs have given their lives for the truth of the only true Triune God and the Holy Scriptures. Tertullian, (160- 220 A.D), the church father who lived in the midst of persecution said, "The blood of the martyrs is the seed of the church." Polycarp (155 A.D.), a disciple of the Apostle John, said to a hushed mob, "Eighty and six years have I served Christ, and He has never done me wrong. How can I blaspheme my King and Savior? I fear not the fire which burns for an hour, and after a little is extinguished . . . why do you delay? Come, do your will." Prior to these martyred saints, the Apostle Paul stated, "For I consider that the sufferings of this present time are not worth comparing with the glory that is to be revealed to us" (Romans 8:18).

Currently, according to some experts a pattern is emerging reminiscent of Jewish persecution in the post war with Germany. "Isolation of, and discrimination against Christians is growing almost geometrically" says Don McAlvany in *The Midnight Herald*. "This is the way it started in Germany against the Jews. As they became more isolated and marginalized by the Nazi propaganda machine, as popular hatred and prejudice against the Jews increased among the German people, wholesale persecution followed. Could this be where the growing anti-Christian consensus in America is taking us?" One person stated, "It didn't start with gas chambers. It started with one party controlling the media, one party controlling the message, one party deciding what is truth, one party censoring speech and silencing opposition. One party divides citizens into us and them and calls on their supporters to harass them. It started when good people turned a blind eye and let it happen." Just recently, college students cried out loudly for the Jewish population to be destroyed by chanting, "From the river to the sea." Despite Hamas' brutal attack on Israel, October 7, 2023, instead of supporting Israel in their battle against Hamas, they are backing the Palestinians.

America is in a truth war. Anytime there is a war, there are causalities. As I wrote in the introduction, "In a war, truth is the first casualty." Why are the sufferers of the gospel willing to die? They believe, as Paul wrote, that what is beyond this world is far greater. Thus, they stand tall in projecting and protecting the truth about God and the Bible. Like I said earlier, humans do not like to hear that they are sinners, and if they don't repent, they will be sentenced to Hell. People don't want to hear that it is only through Jesus that a person can have eternal life (John 14:6). Consequently, men and woman fight for their knowledge of life, their goodness to others, and hold fast that God is only a God of love.

The truth is that God is a God of love but also a God of wrath, judgement, and punishment. The Holy Triune God cannot and will not allow sin to enter into His heaven. This truth war really is around a person, Jesus Christ and His substitutionary atonement and resurrection. People, like Peter and John, today will continue to die holding on to this truth. Why? Because they experienced the resurrection life that Christ has given them. But the paradox in suffering for gospel truth is that the church will flourish, as always, through the seeds of a martyrs' blood.

But what should be the believer's response to suffering? First, we should not be alarmed when suffering comes. First Peter 4:12 gives insight: "Beloved, do not be surprised at the fiery trial when it comes upon you to test you, as though something strange were happening to you." The test is to see if we will trust the Lord in our suffering. Second, what is our attitude toward suffering? The book of James weighs in. James 1:2 states, "Count it all joy, my brothers when you meet trials of various kinds, for you know that the testing of your faith produces steadfastness." Therefore, when suffering comes through trials count it all joy. Let's back track to I Peter 4. He expands on the ideas or attitude to have in suffering. Verse 13 shares "But rejoice insofar as you share Christ's sufferings, that you may also rejoice and be glad when His glory is revealed." Now the climax of rejoicing in suffering is in verse 14, "If you are insulted for the name of Christ, you are blessed, because the Spirit of glory and of God rests upon you." The lesson is simple. Suffering will come as Jesus promised in Matthew 5:10f. Thus, rejoice in the suffering, so we will be identified with Christ as a follower. In Acts 16, Paul and Silas were preaching the good news of Jesus Christ, and a slave girl was delivered from a spirit of divination. Those who were gaining from her fortune-telling dragged Paul and Silas in front of the rulers. The rulers inflected a beating and then threw them into prison and fastened their feet in the stocks. What was their response to this suffering? They were praying and singing hymns (Acts 16:16f).

Paul told young Timothy to "share in suffering as a good solider of Christ Jesus" (2 Timothy 2:3). In his last letter, Paul was passing the torch of the gospel of truth to Timothy. Are we willing to accept the suffering that will come from proclaiming the gospel of truth? As the saints before us, Lord grant us the strength to give you glory when trials come our way for standing for truth that bring an element of suffering.

TESTIFYING TO THE GOSPEL OF GOD'S GRACE

"But I do not account my life of any value nor as precious to
myself, if only I may finish my course and the ministry that
I received from the Lord Jesus, to testify to the
gospel of the grace of God"
(Acts 20:24).

After he was called by the Lord, the Apostle Paul had one goal in life, to preach and teach the grace of God to the Gentiles. This was God's sovereign plan for Paul. Galatians 1:15 says, "But when He who had set me apart before I was born and who called me by His grace, was pleased to reveal His Son to me, in order that I might preach Him among the Gentiles. . ." This call of God upon his life was so intense that nothing mattered more than to fulfill this assignment the Lord had given him.

I have always been impressed by Paul's statement that his life did not matter. It is a most sobering statement. In his letter to the Philippians, Paul shares his impressive Pharisaical resume. His credentials were impeccable (Philippians 3: 3-6). But compared now to his relationship with Christ, all his accomplishments in the flesh were "dung" or "rubbish" (Philippians 3: 8-9). In other words, Jesus was his all. To know Jesus and the power of His resurrection was Paul's primary concern; not what he had achieved in life. This is why he could say, "I do not account my life of any value nor as precious to myself."

Jesus intervened in Saul's life, who would be renamed Paul, while Saul persecuted Christians (Acts 8-9). Saul had nothing to do concerning his salvation. When the light of Jesus blinded Saul, he cried out to Jesus, "Lord, what do you want me to do" (Acts 9:6)? No sinner's prayer was required. No decision to reject or accept what was happening to him. Saul was regenerated by Jesus. The fruit of regeneration is faith and repentance. His change of direction for the rest of his life was by the Lord's grace. This was God's sovereign plan for Saul, who became Paul, before he was born. Why the Lord allowed Saul to persecute so many Christians is a mystery.

Before God intervened into my life at the age of twenty-three, I led a wretched life. Like Saul's life of redemption, my life was transformed by the amazing grace of God. I didn't say a sinner's prayer. I couldn't reject this call upon my life because God changed by heart of stone into a heart of flesh. He put His Spirit in me (Ezekiel 36:26). God gives an outward call to many. But when there is a Holy Spirit call, it is an effective call. In other words, when God makes you born again or born from above (John 3), you are going to have faith and repent of your sin. This is grace.

In addition to the promise of salvation, another promise comes from Philippians 1:6, "He who began a good work in you will bring it to completion." Salvation is all the work of God from being to end. The beginning work is justification, and it is always followed by sanctification – growing in Jesus. It has nothing to do with a decision I might make for God or against God. An old Puritan theologian, John Own, stated, "If salvation were left up to mankind, the possibility would be that no one would choose Christ." In our opening text, this is what Paul is saying. Salvation is the complete work of Jesus Christ.

Paul expresses his desire to complete the call upon his life to share or testify to the grace of God to the Gentile communities. Paul shares his testimony in the beginning of his Galatian letter, in I Timothy 1, and in Philippines 3, while Doctor Luke shares Paul's story in Acts 22. Like Paul, all Christians are to call unbelievers or pagans into a relationship with Jesus, which is to ask them to believe in the death, burial, and resurrection of Jesus according to the scriptures (I Corinthians 15:3-14). It is a call to repent. The first thesis of Martin Luther's "Ninety-Five Theses" says, "When our Lord and Master Jesus Christ said 'Repent,' He intended that the entire life of believers should be repentance."

Like Paul stated, unless we are willing to die to ourselves, none of this can happen. From obedience to Scripture, we give our resources to a church that desires to see people won to Jesus. As the Holy Spirit leads, we tell our story of grace to others. We give the outward call, then Jesus' sovereign will gives the inward call through the Holy Spirit (John 1:12-13). As Paul stated to young Timothy, he suffered for the elect (II Timothy 2: 9-10). He didn't know who the Lord elected for salvation but he preached knowing that some will come to faith and repentance. As I wrote earlier, Charles Spurgeon said that he had no idea who are the elect, so he preaches "whosoever" will come. Let us continue to pray that the Lord will come into whomever you are praying for. Don't pray that this person will come to Jesus but that Jesus will come to the person. Pray that this person will experience the amazing grace of our Lord.

A month ago, I testified about the good news of Jesus to a dying friend. A friend of mine from high school developed a brain tumor. He was successful throughout his life. In fact, he played and worked for major league baseball for fifty-years. Another high school classmate called me when he learned of the declining health of our friend. He said we need to make a road trip to see if our dying friend knows Jesus Christ. I felt the urgency as well, and the next day we drove five hours to spend time with our former classmate. On the way down, I prayed, "Lord, make a way for me to share the Gospel with my friend." Upon arriving, we were met by his two beautiful labs, and his wife. Entering the house, we found our friend in his recliner. He was not able to hear well, so I sat in a chair close to him so he could hear me. We began talking about our times playing baseball together from little league through high school. Then I brought up the baseball cards we collected while growing up. I mentioned Bobby Richardson and Mickey Mantle. "Praise the Lord," I said to myself. Just prior to Mantle dying, I remembered the story of Richardson sharing Christ with him. This was my segue to share the gospel. I shared the gospel message with him. Our friend said he knew Christ and he associated with Christians on his major league teams. The conversation moved on to another topic. After returning home, I emailed him the Roman Road to salvation to remind him of our conversation. His brain tumor caused lapses of memory and concentration. I am sad to say, as I write today, the Lord called him home. I never observed his life to see the character of Christ displayed. I can only go by what he shared with me. Hopefully, he knows Jesus. I pray he has and he will experience the amazing grace of our Lord in Heaven.

TOLERANCE OF THE TRUTH

"For certain persons have crept in unnoticed, those who were long beforehand marked out for this condemnation, ungodly persons who turn the grace of our God into licentiousness and deny our only Master and Lord, Jesus Christ" (Jude 1:4).

"Our lives are shaped by the 'god' we worship – whether the God of the Bible or some substitute deity."
(Nancy Pearcey –*Total Truth*)

"Truth is that which is consistent with the mind, will, character, glory, and being of God. Even more to the point: Truth is the self-expression of God."
(John MacArthur, *The Truth War*)

Years ago, people could debate ideas yet part on good terms. In other words, they could tolerate a different opinion. Today, if one does not agree with a person's opinion, then he is classified as a hate monger or worse. Relativism has become a person's god. The thinking of the relativist, "It is my thought, so it must be true. And who are you to disagree with me?" Nancy Pearcy is correct in writing that one is shaped by the "god" one worships. Although not admitting it, most worship the god of self. Even though an opinion might be a lie, they believe it as truth. This is where many Americans are today: Intolerance must be digested by the tolerant, but tolerance is indigestible to the intolerant.

The nation's 2024 Presidential election has two stark differences on how to run America. For example, the far left will not tolerate drilling for oil or natural gas. They adhere to the pseudo-climate change argument that fossil fuel will destroy our nation. They will not tolerate the idea of first building an infrastructure to support environmental energy. We can have both without eliminating what we have used for energy for centuries. However, this will not be tolerated. Whoever controls the energy has the power and control of its citizens.

Guinness points out in *A Time for Truth*, the relativist banner, "Truth is dead; knowledge is power." He highlights Fredrick Nietzsche's influence on the life of Picasso. Picasso's mantra was, "Truth cannot exist . . . truth does not exist. I am God, I am God." Nietzsche is famous for his statement, "God is dead." It made headlines on the *Time* magazine cover; on April 8, 1966, "Is God Dead?" The erosion of the existence of God began in the sixties, and almost sixty years later some believe God is dead. The opening ceremony of the 2024 summer Olympics in Paris had a drag queen performance of Jesus' "Last Supper" painting by Leonardo da Vinci. Doesn't it seem odd that no other faith is mocked or ridiculed? There is no tolerance for Christianity in the world. The majority only worship the gods of their minds. Sadly, most think the God of all creation does not exist.

The book of Jude says some have crept into the church unnoticed to teach false doctrine. This has happened in churches across America, and the pseudo-truth teachers and leaders have made their way into the universities and into the political arena as well. Their politically correct agenda will not tolerate the truth as defined by MacArthur," Truth is the self-expression of God."

When Jesus taught that He was God, (at least 38 references in the Bible of that fact), the Pharisees could not stomach such a heretical statement. Jesus stated, "Most assuredly, I say to you, before Abraham was, I AM" (John 8:58). The Old Testament scholars, Pharisees, and scribes, knew that 'I AM' was God, because when Moses met God at the burning bush (Exodus 3), He told Moses, to tell Pharaoh that the "I AM has sent him to free the Israelites." Jesus' truth statement, I AM God, could not be tolerated, so the religious leaders had Him executed on a cross.

Colson describes the worldview in our culture from his book, *The Good Life*: "No such thing as truth! Tolerance is god! Diversity rules at all cost." Worldview thinkers are intolerant of the narrowness of biblical teaching. Thus, they can reprimand an employee for having a Bible on the workplace desk. The Koran, far eastern religious literature, and other faiths are recognized in public, but not Christianity's Bible. The tolerance of truth has vanished. If the politically correct language is not expressed, or agreement around abortion, gay marriage and lifestyle, and that any religion will allow someone entrance into heaven, a Christian today will be called narrow-minded, fundamentalist, ignorant, and not relevant in today's culture. Intolerance rules the landscape – agree or be bullied or worse. Tolerance for truth cannot be grasped by the intolerant. Many times, in this book I have stated that life of babies must be protected in the womb; children must not be able to decide what gender they desire; our nation's borders must be closed, and allow only those who are processed legally into our country. The far-left and the unregenerate population's position is they will not tolerate this truth. To tolerate truth means they will have to change their thinking and lifestyle.

John MacArthur has it right when he writes the following:

Lies That Humans Believe:

1. Life is random.
2. Truth is relative.
3. People are basically good.

4. Everyone can change if he chooses to.
5. The goal of life is self-satisfaction.

The Truth is Opposite from the Above:

1. God is sovereign and nothing is random.
2. The Bible is absolute truth.
3. All people are basically sinful.
4. Only Christ can change your life.
5. Selfless submission to Christ is the goal of life.

How about you, which list do you embrace?

UNITY IN THE CHURCH THROUGH GRACE

"But grace was given to each one of us according to the measure of Christ's gift" (Ephesians 4:7).

Church growth will be constant when there is unity in the body of believers. The early church declared that the true church had three distinct marks:

1. The gospel was preached.
2. The two ordinances of the church, baptism and the Lord's Supper were observed.
3. That church discipline was included in the church's governing documents.

These sign-posts were designed for the church body to agree upon, and to take seriously the implementation of each. In doing so, the church could remain united.

A more recent teaching on church unity is by Larry Osborne from his book *The Unity Factor*. The author cites three areas the church must carryout to maintain unity:

1. Doctrinally – the church's belief system around the doctrines of the Bible.
2. Philosophically – an agreed belief in the church's vision and mission.
3. Relationally – to uphold loving, encouraging, and disciplining one another.

Ephesians 4 highlights both distinctive marks from the different eras mentioned above. Verse seven in our focus text cites a key word "but," which could mean "on the other hand." It reflects what has been said in the previous verses concerning unity. The verse moves the reader from "all" for unity in the church to "each one" in the body. Each one has a relational responsibility to maintain unity. Grace in our text is not for salvation but for enabling. The gift is measured out by God's sovereign grace decree on each person. As John MacArthur writes in his commentary on Ephesians, "God gives electing grace, equipping grace, and enabling grace." Our enabling grace gift is used for the building up of the body, and to keep unity in the church.

In 1 Corinthians 12: 4-7, Apostle Paul states each one is given the manifestation of the Spirit for the "common good" of the body. Romans 12:6-8, I Corinthians 12: 8-10, and Ephesians 4:11 list spiritual gifts. But each gift is given out differently and in different degrees. For example, no two teachers or preachers have the same abilities. 1Peter 4:10-11 puts one's gifts for unity in perspective: "As each has received a gift, use it to serve one another, as good stewards of God's varied grace. . . in order that in everything God may be glorified through Jesus Christ."

A subtitle for Ephesians is "unity in the church." Paul's letter highlights what Jesus' "High Priestly Prayer" stated in John 17. Jesus prayed: "The glory that you have given me I have given to them, that they may be one even as we are one, I in them and you in me, that they may become perfectly one, so the world may know that you sent me and loved them even as you loved me (vv22-23).

Unity is the key to evangelism when a church is reaching out to the world. The church must be one in Christ. Why invite someone to a church that has no peace? Of course, there will be differences, not everyone is going to think alike, but everyone will be on the same page doctrinally. They will hold to the virgin birth of Jesus, the bodily resurrection of Jesus, Jesus substitutionary atonement, that there is a Satan and a Hell, that Jesus is the only way to heaven, that God creates genders, and designed marriage between a man and a woman, and the Scriptures are without error. If someone is not on the same doctrinal wavelength of thinking, then a person should leave the church and find a liberal church.

Paul was clear in this letter to the Ephesians that unity should be made a top priority within the church, but not through sacrificing doctrinal purity (chapters 1-3). He began this letter teaching doctrine in the first three chapters. He followed doctrine with a beautiful doxology at the end of chapter three. In chapters 4-6, he teaches how to maintain unity within the church by each member "walking in a manner worthy of your calling to which you have been called." Martyn Lloyd-Jones in his Ephesians commentary states the word "worthy," means "to balance your doctrine with your relational walk with Jesus and one another."

A growing conservative church places doctrine as a top priority. The church members live out walking in a doctrinal manner together for the glory of the Lord. The church's early theological fathers, and the more recent theologians, they place doctrine and relationships as the ingredients for church unity.

Through an observation of churches in America, one will find that those churches that are liberal in doctrine are the ones declining in membership; whereas, the conservative churches are growing. For example, one of the hallmarks of liberal churches are women pastors on staff or as senior pastors. Plus, some non-biblical churches perform gay marriages, and support women's reproductive rights, and transgenderism. One denomination in America has lost over a million members because of these doctrinal positions. Bottom line, any church that allows the world's system of belief into their church is one that the Lord will not bless.

A unified church is like the Aspen tree one finds in the Rockies and other cold climate regions. While on sabbatical in the Rockies, I was drawn to these unique trees. Their light-colored bark, dotted with black spots, and their golden leaves beautified the Rocky Mountains. The root system of these trees is what makes them intriguing. Even though Aspen trees stand independently tall (50 - 100 feet), their root systems interlock. This interlocking strengthens the trees and enables them to withstand strong winds and snowstorms. Aspens are termed "clonal colony" trees because the root system of one tree reproduces itself numerous times. Likewise, the church's root system interlocks the membership in its faith in the Lord and love for one another. Also, like the Aspen tree, the church body is called to reproduce itself. The membership is commanded to make disciples. One tree may have other trees sprout from its root system 98 to 138 feet from the parent tree. Likewise, in the church, each person learning and implementing the discipleship process will assist in making disciples.

Church unity is built by God's grace through keeping doctrine and relationships as primary in the life of the church. My friends, go to a church that has clear foundational biblical teaching, and the members are using their enabling spiritual gifts for the common good of the body. Yes, worship in a unified church!

Universality of the Truth

"The sum of your word is truth, and every one of your righteous rules endures forever" (Psalm 119:160).

"Let the lie come into the world, even dominate the world, but not through me." (Alexander Solzhenitsyn)

One of the great movie dialogues is between naval lawyer Kaffee and Marine Colonel Jessup during a trial to prove that "Code Reds" (a hazing technique to motivate slack soldiers) were authorized by Colonel Jessup. The heated courtroom dialogue with Colonel Jessup on the witness stand:

> Kaffee: Colonel Jessup, did you order the Code Red?
> Judge Randolph: You don't have to answer that question!
> Colonel Jessup: I'll answer the question! [*to Kaffee*]
> Colonel Jessup: You want answers?
> Kaffee: I think I'm entitled to.
> Colonel Jessup: You want answers?
> Kaffee: I want the truth!
> Colonel Jessup: You can't handle the truth!

Like in the movie, *A Few Good Men*, it is hard to uncover the truth in America. Colonel Jessup was living a lie, as I will explain later, he was a true narcissist. The lawyer, Kaffee, in the movie wanted the truth. I believe deep down most people want the truth.

Truth, Veritas, the motto for Harvard University really has become a cliché or worn-out slogan. This giant university once touted, "The end of education is to know the Lord Jesus Christ who is eternal life." Truth is no longer a highwater mark of these higher leaning institutions and the so-called places of worship. Consequently, cultures cannot handle the truth because they are believing the lies that flow from universities and the far-left government. The truth is that the Triune God is universal in *being* the Truth. All that He has said through His Word, the Bible, is that all He has created and the way He created all is truth. God's truth is universal in nature. That is, it is true for all creation. As the Psalmist wrote in 119, "all your words are true. . ." God is the truth in the Western hemisphere as He is in the Eastern hemisphere. What has happened to truth? In the East, it was trampled upon by socialism, and in the West by materialism. People have permitted the government and materialism to be their god.

Is it not strange in America that there are advocates clamoring for socialism? Have they not seen the spiritual wasteland that socialism creates in other countries? Here in America, our country is becoming like a desert. We are trying to build a country on an ideology of sand. The prophetic voice of Jesus in Matthew 7 could be a reality in America. The Nation is building on a foundation of sand which will wash away one day. Instead, as the word says in Matthew 7, we should be building on the Rock, which is Jesus Christ.

In his 1978 commencement address at Harvard, Solzhenitsyn stated, "We have placed too much hope in politics and social reforms, only to find out that we were being deprived of our most precious possession: our spiritual life." Politics and social ideas have hardened the hearts of most individuals towards a spiritual life. Like Colonel

Jessup, I have family members who are trapped in a narcissistic lifestyle. Duke University Health describes such a person by using the acrostic "Special Me:"

1. Sense of self-importance.
2. Preoccupation with power, beauty, or success.
3. Entitled.
4. Can only be around people who are important or special.
5. Interpersonally exploitative for their own gain.
6. Arrogant
7. Lack of empathy.
8. Must be admired.
9. Envious of others or believe that others are envious of them.

This socially unhealthy attitude has captured so many in the United States. This attitude about self has caused a barrier to keep the spiritual life out. Listen to what Jesus says to the narcissist:

1. The narcissist says, "Follow your heart." Jesus said, "Follow Me."
2. The narcissist says, "Be true to yourself." Jesus said, "Whoever wants to be My disciple, must deny himself."
3. The narcissist says, "Believe in yourself." Jesus said, "Believe in Me."
4. The narcissist says, "Live your truth." Jesus said, "I am the Truth."
5. The narcissist says, "As long as you are happy." Jesus said, "What will it profit a man if he gains the world and loses his soul."

The socialist nations, those governed only by the government, are blinded to God, and many socialist Americans have developed cataracts which have blurred their vision of God. The United States has two polar opposite views of governing her citizenry. One view wants freedom and safety for the populace. This includes using the God given energy supply of oil and propane, closing the borders, allowing parents to weigh in on their children's decision of being a transgender, and increasing law enforcement because they understand evil. The totally opposite is the other viewpoint that wants government control by enforcing a climate control agenda, not allowing parents to have total control of their children, to reduce law enforcement by believing that better education, housing, and jobs will reduce the crime rate. This shows a total misunderstanding of the heart of man. Man is sinful, and he will act according to his nature. That nature is sinful. One stands for true liberty, the other stands for a pseudo-freedom. One stands for Godly principles, the other doesn't recognize the spiritual teachings from God.

The universal truth is that God must, and He will, rule His creation. Creation must come under submission to the Creator. In Psalm 117, the Psalmist declares, "Praise the LORD, all you nations! Praise Him all you peoples! For His merciful kindness is great toward us, And the truth of the LORD endures forever." Will our nation hold to lies or gravitate towards the truth? "Let the lie come into the world, even dominate the world, but not through me." Are you living the lie or the universal truth – Jesus is God, the God of total Truth, and that His truth applies to all nations? Around the world 1+1= 2; similarly, around the world, Jesus is the universal Truth.

VICTORY IN THE FUTURE BY GRACE

"Therefore, preparing your minds for action, and being sober minded, set your hope fully on the grace that will be brought to you at the revelation of Jesus" (I Peter 1:13).

The hymn I favor the most is "Victory in Jesus." The chorus reads, "Oh, victory in Jesus, my Savior forever; He sought me and bought me with His redeeming blood; He loved me 'ere I knew Him and all my love is due Him; He plunged me to victory beneath the cleansing flood." How grateful we should be that Jesus sought us and then bought us through shedding His blood on the Cross. As the first stanza in the hymn states, I am a "wretch." First Peter reminds us of the Lord's great love for wretches like us.

In our focus text, the "Therefore" in the text takes us back to the first twelve verses of chapter one of First Peter. Here Peter writes in 1:3, "Jesus has caused us to be born again to a living hope through the resurrection of Jesus Christ from the dead, to an inheritance that is imperishable." This future hope that we have is a military expression that we have victory in obtaining the inheritance promised to us. We have victory in our present salvation over sin and death. Now we have victory in the hope or certainty we have in our future with Jesus. All of this we owe to Jesus because as the text states, "Jesus caused us to be born again." He did the work of regeneration to make us born again. If Jesus had not "caused" us to be transformed, then it would have never happened.

Just as grace through faith from the Lord gave us salvation (Ephesians 2:8-9), our future grace of hope will give us our promised inheritance. God's grace gave us faith to believe in Jesus. The hope we have is like faith, we are trusting God for our future promise. Peter uses the word "fully" to say Christians should hope in a decisive or full way without any reservations concerning the future promises of God.

Peter writes for us to "prepare our minds for action." In other words, "gird up," or "tighten the belt," to prepare for an action. The NKJV says "gird up the loins of your mind." When an Israelite went into battle, he had to pull his garment up around his waist and tie it snuggly so he could run to fight.

Set your mind on Jesus not on things here on earth (Colossians 3:1-2) is to tighten your thinking on the things of God. The devil will try to convince you that things here are more important than things that Jesus has promised. Just like he did with Adam and Eve, Satan attacks the mind first. "Surely, you won't die," he stated (Genesis 3:4. . .). This is why we are encouraged to set our minds on the Spirit and not on the flesh (Romans 8: 5-8).

He says to "keep sober in spirit or be sober-minded." John MacArthur's commentary on I Peter shares, "This literally means not to become intoxicated which is to lose control of thought and action." Our minds should be set on Jesus' return. At the revelation of Jesus' reappearing, we will receive grace to be in the presence of Jesus. All Christians should wait eagerly for His return. Our eyes must be set on Him and not this world. If we are not looking for Jesus, then how deeply in love are we with Him? When I first started dating my wife, I counted every day until our wedding day. That same enthusiasm should be in desiring to see Jesus. For through Jesus and by way of the cross, we are victorious because all our sins are forgiven. By way of the empty tomb, we are victorious because we know that we will see Jesus in heaven.

Hebrews 11:16 reads, "Instead, they were longing for a better country, a heavenly one. Therefore, God is not ashamed to be called their God, for He has prepared a city for them." What a future a believer has to look forward to! A city has been prepared for them because they are longing for a better country. Verse 10 says, "whose architect and builder is God." See how God has worked for us. We are not building this city, but God is designing and constructing it for us. Are you yearning for this city that God has created for us more than you desire the things of this world? What a victorious future we have through God's grace.

An 1890 hymn, "Victory Through Grace," by John R. Sweney highlights our victorious battle through grace. Stanza one:

> Conquering now and still to conquer, Rideth a King in His might, /
> Leading the host all the faithful into the midst of the fight/
> See them with courage advancing, clad in their brilliant array/
> Shouting the name of their Leader, hear them exultingly say,
> Chorus:
> Not to the strong is the battle, not to the swift is the race, yet to the true and the faithful victory is promised through grace.

VOICE OF THE TRUTH

"... and for this I have come into the world, to testify to the
truth. Everyone who is of the truth hears My voice"
(John 18:37).

"See to it that no one takes you captive (carries you off) through
hallow and deceptive philosophy; which depends on human
tradition and the basic principles of this world
rather than on Christ" (Colossians 2:8).

Are the voices of this world "carrying you off" into darkness without your realizing it? Chuck Colson in his book, *The Good Life*, stated, "America has grown accustomed to the dark, they don't even know the lights are out." Which voice are you hearing – your voice or the voice of God? The voice of relativism or the voice of truth? Do you listen to the voice of socialism or the voice of capitalism? Static makes hearing difficult. Through all the hissing noises in our society, who are you going to trust? Who has remained consistently trustworthy and faithful? Has socialism? Examine the economic failures, the imprisonment of those who didn't follow the government's agenda, (i.e. Solzhenitsyn in Russia), and the squelching of religion.

Has relativism whose cousins are humanism and secularism been faithful and trustworthy? Only the most powerful opinions will surface to be heard and followed. The three "isms" fail to capture the state of the human nature. Everyone is a sinner. Sinners lie to achieve their desired goals. Many times, they don't know they are lying, because it is part of their unregenerate nature. Those listening believe the lie is truth. The liar is part of the devil's kingdom, because he is the father of lies. What follows lies is deception. Liars are deceivers making others think they are doing the right thing. Deception finally gets one entangled in the liar's web of ideology, philosophy, and theology. Basically, God is dead, and humans are the gods. You have been held captive through deception; you have become the spoil.

Let's add Jesus' voice to the list of voices. Jesus was crystal clear in His statement, "Everyone who is of the truth hears my voice." In other words, if you have a relationship with Jesus, you will hear His voice of truth. Can the voice of God be trusted? Guinness makes God's trustworthiness HD-sharp in his book, *Time for Truth: Living free in a world of Lies, Hype, and Spin*, "God may be trusted because He is the True One. He is true, He acts truly, and He speaks truly-for Christians, most clearly and fully in Jesus, His effective, spoken Word. Therefore, God's truthfulness is foundational for His trustworthiness." Hebrews 1:1-3 weighs in on Guinness' statement; listen to the writer, "Long ago, at many times and in many ways, God spoke to our fathers by the prophets, but in these last days He spoke to us by His Son, whom He appointed the heir of all things, through whom also He created the world. He is the radiance of the glory of God and the exact imprint of His nature, and He upholds the universe by the word of His power." Jesus is the exact imprint of God, so His voice can be trusted.

How can one have ears to hear the teachings of Jesus? As Jesus shared with the Pharisee, Nicodemus, one must be born again (John 3). A regenerated heart removes the cataracts from one's eyes and the hearing impairments so the voice of the Truth can resonate with the person. Once hearing the Truth, the new believer abides in truth, and the Truth sets the person free (John 8:31-32). However, once born again, some Christians develop apathy towards hearing God's truth.

Review from a previous chapter from Hebrews, which cites the problems some have. Hebrews 2:1 says believers "must pay much closer attention to what we have heard, lest we *drift* away." The hearing is captured by the loudest voice in the room because the person is not in the Word of God. If we are not in the Word daily, we don't know what to believe in the marketplace. Who tells the truth and who spouts off lies? Besides drifting, one must heed the command in Hebrews 3:13, *do not harden* your heart. The text reads, "Today if you hear His voice, do not harden your hearts as in rebellion." Some become so absorbed in the world's thinking, their hearts slowly become hardened to the Word of God. They no longer take the Bible literally or as inerrant. Finally, the Hebrew writer in 5:11 states that some have become *dull* of hearing. Because of this, they have not become teachers. I don't hear well out of my left ear. I'm always asking my wife, "what did you say?" The dullness in hearing the Word of God allows the person to be easy prey by Satan, the father of lies. Therefore, whether you *drift* from God's voice, or disobey his command of *don't* harden your heart, or be *dull* of hearing the voice of God through the Word, you are in danger of being "carried away" into a philosophy of the world. Not only that, but you can also become discouraged, disillusioned, dissatisfied, or defeated in life. Satan has you in his web of lies to destroy your joy, peace, faith, and love in life. The Christian must always fight any tendency towards apathy.

However, the good news is that the born-again believer can discern what is truth and what is a lie. This person knows whom to trust. The believer hears the voice of truth because the person knows the One who is the Truth – Jesus. Thus, the individual stays tuned in to Him.

WISDOM FROM THE GRACE OF GOD

"For our proud confidence is this: the testimony of our conscience, that in holiness and godly sincerity, not in fleshly wisdom but in the grace of God, we have conducted ourselves in the world, and especially toward you"
(2 Corinthians 1:12 (NASB 1995).

The Apostle Paul gives a warning to the church in Colossae, "See to it that no one takes you captive (carries you away – NAS) by philosophy and empty deceit, according to human tradition, according to the elementary spirits of the world and not according to Christ" (Colossians 2:8). Everything we hear from the world, must be reviewed by Scripture. Many today are looking for life guidance through astrology. If the stars aren't in alignment, they won't marry a certain person, take a job opportunity, or make other life decisions.

Plus, worldly "woke" ideas of marriage, gender transitioning, open boarders, abortion, position on supporting Israel, and other "woke" philosophies are not in line with biblical teachings. Paul wrote young Timothy and shared with him how in the last days there will be times of difficulty: lovers of self and money, proud, arrogant, abusive, disobedient to their parents, ungrateful, unholy, heartless, unappeasable, slanderous, without self-control. brutal, not loving food, treacherous, reckless, swollen with conceit, lovers of pleasure rather than lovers of God (2Timothy 3:1-5). The book of Judges ends, ". . . Everyone did what was right in his own eyes." (Judges 21:25b)

Paul stated that his "boasting" (ESV) or "proud confidence" was in the testimony of his conscience. Conscience has the concept of knowing oneself. His conscience is guided by the word of God. This is why Paul said, "We behave in the world with holiness and godly sincerity." This way of thinking doesn't come from the world or "fleshly wisdom" but from "the grace of God." Paul's boasting is not about what he has accomplished, but how God has worked through him. His conscience was clear and clean because he relied on the work of the Spirit, not from the flesh (Romans 8).

"Holiness" in the text indicates moral purity or pure motives.

Godly "sincerity" means to inspect. In my home, we have an antique rocking chair. In one of our moves, one arm of the chair developed a hair line break. We super glued the crack. Unless you put the arm under a bright light you cannot see the hair line fracture on the rocking chair arm. Paul said to put his life under the light for inspection to see the purity of his life. Fleshly wisdom cannot produce the purity Paul is addressing about his life.

Paul made it clear in I Corinthians 15:10 NASB 1995, "But by the grace of God I am what I am, and His grace toward me did not prove vain; but I labored even more then all of them, yet not I, but the grace of God with me." God's grace gave Paul's purity, thus a clear conscience. He magnifies the grace of God throughout his writings. The Apostle takes no credit for his accomplishments or his pure mindset. It is all about God's grace.

From his Damascus road intervention by Jesus and throughout his ministry, Paul continued to rely on the grace of God. The grace from God is what others saw in his life and what others read about his life from his works.

Do you see in your life God's grace working through you, or are they observing how you depend on the world's philosophies? Are you being developed or sanctified by God's grace? Or is your grace what Bonhoeffer called "cheap grace?"

Dietrich Bonhoeffer, the great German pastor, theologian, martyr, and spy was asked in 1943 how it was possible for the church to sit back and let Hitler seize absolute power. His firm answer: "It was the teaching of cheap grace." He stated, "Cheap grace is the preaching of forgiveness without requiring repentance, baptism without church discipline, communion without confession, absolution without personal confession. Cheap grace is grace without discipleship, grace without the cross, and grace without Jesus Christ." We live in a time and culture that not only teaches "cheap grace" but praises it.

Our world screams, "Look at me!" But grace yells back, "Look at what God has done." As Martin Luther wrote, "If grace depends on our cooperation then it is no longer grace." Paul told the Corinthians to look at what God did through him by His grace.

How about you? Do you boast in your own fleshly strength and worldly wisdom or in God's sovereign grace upon your life? One could spell Jesus - GRACE.

WEIGHT OF THE TRUTH

"Lead me in Your truth and teach me, For You are the God of my salvation; For You I wait all the day" (Psalm 25:5).

"One word of truth outweighs the entire world"
- Aleksandr Solzhenitsyn

"Living in truth is the secret of living free."
Os Guinness

The weight of truth will transform a person, a community, and a country. Weight means the importance, moment, consequence, or effective influence. Jesus used the word in Matthew 23:23. Jesus said, "Woe to you, scribes and Pharisees, hypocrites! For you tithe mint and dill and cumin, and have neglected the weightier (*more important*) matters of the law: justice, and mercy and faithfulness. These you ought to have done, without neglecting the others." Jesus said that tithing goods is fine, but the more important matters or weightier matters are what they have neglected. Truth is the most important matter a person can bring to a discussion. Lies weigh a person down with the individual's unbridled deception. In order to maintain the deception, more lies need to be laid to create a pseudo-stable foundation of dishonesty.

We have observed the cracks and crumbled foundation in education's strategy to deceive the American public. For example, some have stated that, Horace Mann, the Father of American Education, in 1837 desired to remove Christ from the classroom. Likewise, John Dewy stated in 1928, "Christianity is the principle problem that needs to be solved in education; the great task of the school is to counteract and transform those domestic and neighborhood tendencies . . . the influence of home and church. In 1915, Antonio Gramsci stated, "Socialism is precisely the religion that must overwhelm Christianity . . . In the New Order, socialism will triumph by first capturing the culture via infiltration of schools, universities, churches and the media by transforming the consciousness of society . . ." These quotes and numerous others all support the State's deception to sway the thinking of America's children towards godlessness. The false teaching of a socialist state shackles a nation. However, truth is the weightier teachings from Christ, and His doctrines must be taught in the classroom, and lived out in a nation. Currently, a few states want children in the fifth grade through the twelfth grade to be taught the Bible in the educational system. Plus, some states desire the Ten Commandments to be on display in the school. It will remain be seen if these Christian aspirations will come to fruition.

Now, examine the current facts in America. The educational system has made science the god of the nation. Even some liberal preachers have swallowed the lie of evolution by calling creation, "theistic evolution." God's speaking creation into being causes the liberal educator's ears to hurt. The weightier truth is that God created the world out of nothing.

Another example, from the so-called learned, is that they say humanity being called sinners is heresy. They believe people are basically good, and individuals evolve towards a higher good, despite the headlines of newspapers and other media reports of murders, rapes, and thievery. The liberal thinkers and churches hold onto a straw-truth of goodness. Human goodness is their highwater mark, but these eventually prove to be lies. The liberal thinkers believe by giving a person better housing, education, and jobs that the crime rate will decrease. They forget or do not acknowledge that we humans are sinners. As Jeremiah 17:9 reads, "The heart is deceitful above all things, and desperately sick (wicked, incurable), who can understand it?" The weightier truth or most important truth is to recognize that we humans have a **s**elfish **i**ndependent **n**ature. Only Christ will make our educational system and nation better.

When humans become the center of their existence, then each person decides what is best for himself. For example, the clarion call is for women to have the right to abort the life they are housing. The woman sees this baby as simply a blob of cells, not a life. Yet the more important truth teaches that the fetus, which means "little one" in Latin, will develop over time to become a mature baby. It is not a blob of cells, but a person. Abortion can produce a life time of guilt in the woman's heart. However, the woman is willing to opt for the convenience of abortion despite the guilt.

The polar opposite is the Christian view of truth that totally outweighs the lies of the educational system and the liberal church. Os Guinness stated, "One word of truth sets the person free," and he is free to cry out to God to lead in His truth and to teach this truth. Jesus stated true-truth, ". . . Come to me, all of you who are weary and carry heavy burdens, and I will give you rest. Take my yoke upon you. Let me teach you, because I am humble and gentle at heart, and you will find rest for your souls. For my yoke is easy to bear, and the burden I give you is light" (Matthew 11:28-30 - NLT). Sin hangs on one's shoulders, it darkens the heart. The burden to live a sin filled life is empty, unfulfilling, and never satisfying, It is like filling your car's gas tank; it always needs to be refilled. But Jesus expresses a compassionate plea to come to Him, and you will find rest for your soul from a sinful life. I hold to what John Newton wrote, "I have lived a satisfied life." How many can say what Newton wrote?

The weight of goodness is crushed in acknowledging one's sinful nature. The weariness of being a god is erased by allowing Jesus to be the God of one's life. Aleksandr Solzhenitsyn was right in saying, "The weight of one word of truth outweighs the entire world" – that one word of truth is Jesus. He stated, "I am the truth" (John 14:6), and apostle John wrote, Jesus is "full of grace and truth" (John 1:14).

X-FACTOR IN CHRISTIANITY IS GRACE

"The grace of our Lord Jesus Christ be with you all"
(2 Thessalonians 3:18).

There have been numerous, maybe hundreds, of books written on the biblical topic of grace. In addition, plentiful hymns have been penned with the theme of grace. Probably the most popular, by all churches, is "Amazing Grace." All of Paul's letters include the word grace somewhere in the content.

Paul was coined, "the apostle of grace." There are 131 uses of grace in the ESV bible. 124 of the verses are in the New Testament, and Paul uses the word 86 times in his writings. Thus, two-thirds of the word is used by Paul (John Piper). To him, grace was the x-factor of his faith.

X-factor is defined by the *Oxford Dictionary* as "something truly special about a person or thing, a quality that's hard to put into words." Grace, underserved favor towards us by God, is difficult to comprehend. We know the definition of grace, but it is hard to explain how grace does its transforming work. For example, salvation is by grace alone, faith alone, in Christ alone. We experience the regenerative work of Christ of being born again, but we cannot explain the mysterious workings of grace to bring salvation to fruition.

X-Factor in Christianity is Grace

Grace enables believers to perform gifts of the Spirit. Paul was clear in I Corinthians 12 about spiritual gifts. For Paul, his gifts were preaching and teaching the gospel of grace to the Gentiles. In I Corinthians 15:10, he magnifies the working of grace in his ministry. "But by the grace of God I am what I am, and his grace toward me was not in vain. On the contrary, I worked harder than any of them, though it was not I, but the grace of God." As I wrote earlier, the most sobering verse to me, that Paul stated to the elders of Ephesus as he was departing is, "But I do not account my life of any value nor as precious to myself, if only I may finish my course and the ministry that I received from the Lord Jesus, to testify to the gospel of grace of God" (Acts 20:24). The x-factor of grace was truly on Paul's heart.

Christians must realize that it is the Lord's work in us that allows us to perform in ministry for His glory. The x-factor in us is the grace of God working through us.

Unlike Paul, many allow the flesh to lead them to take credit for what they do in ministry. But we must always remember, as Paul did, that grace is actively working in us. The grace working in us is what we should be testifying to as Paul did. I don't know about you, I have trouble not counting my life of any value or precious to myself. There is always some form of pride that wants to be acknowledged. Jesus said it clearly that we must deny ourselves and take up our cross daily. As the theologian of old, John Owen, wrote that the mortification of our sin is a lifelong process. He wrote, "Be killing sin or sin will be killing you." Evidently, Paul learned how to put the sin of pride in self to death.

On the other hand, Nebuchadnezzar was a proud king. He said, "Look at me." He thought a lot about himself. He saw himself as smart, important, and strong. All that he did, he thought was great, and he wanted everyone to agree with him. He said, "Is not this great Babylon, which I have built by my mighty power as a royal residence and for the glory of my majesty" (Daniel 4:30)? Yes, "look at me" was his mantra. Through a dream Nebuchadnezzar realized God's favor upon his kingship. He said, "Now I, Nebuchadnezzar, praise and extol and honor the King of heaven, for all His works are right and His ways are just; and those who walk in pride He is able to humble" (Daniel 4:37).

Grace is like the wind. We know the wind is blowing by seeing the leaves sway, or by feeling a breeze upon our cheeks. We recognize this as wind but we don't know exactly how the wind is created or works. Yes, we see the effects of grace when a life is transformed or watching a believer minister in a certain capacity.

Take me for example. I used to stutter. I could not say my name unless I first stated, "My name is." When God called me to preach, the stuttering left. I can't explain it, but grace manifested itself.

As Paul completed his letter to the church at Thessalonica, he desired all to experience God's grace and to give God the glory for providing grace to their lives. We need to follow suit.

X-FACTOR OF THE TRUTH

"I am the way, the truth, and the life, and no one can come to the Father expect through Me (John 14:6).

"Jesus is the difference Maker."

In my pre-teen and teen years, I collected major league baseball cards. One could buy a box of hundred cards for a dollar in the late fifties and early sixties. My collection today, if I still had the cards, is valued at approximately forty thousand dollars. I remember buying a Willie Mays card from a friend for seventy-five cents. That was not chump change in the day. What made my collection so valuable were the "difference makers" in the collection. Players like Mantle, Maris, Robinson, Kaline, Clemente, Aaron, Ford, Koufax, and Drysdale are just a few examples of the difference makers in the collection. But who is the all-time great difference maker in life? It is not a sports figure, philosopher, theologian, entrepreneur, writer, speaker, or politician. None of these! The greatest difference maker was and is Jesus Christ. Jesus is the X- Factor in life. Jesus has the most significant impact on the outcome of true-truth because He is the Truth.

I married at nineteen and divorced when I was twenty-three. The first week of the marriage breakup, I found myself on a dirt road with tall tobacco plants on each side of the car. On that cold night in southside Virginia, I cried out to God. I thought I had life by the tail. High School was a huge success. I had decent grades, lettered in three sports, and dated a cheerleader. Then I married in college and played basketball. We had a daughter who was a delight. We both graduated from college, and we were beginning to start a somewhat normal life. The marriage road was rocky, but I thought we would make it with both of us working. Suddenly, the rug was pulled out from under me. She had found another. We separated and eventually divorced. But that night on the tobacco road my life changed. Jesus found me! Ever since that night, I have followed Jesus. Not perfectly, of course, but He grew me into who I am today. Even though I divorced, His grace called me to preach, and I did for forty-three years. Though some have disagreed about my calling to preach, I had no control over my circumstance, and I wasn't a Christian at the time of my separation. I remarried at age twenty-five and we have walked together for forty-nine years. Through it all, yes, Jesus became and is my X-Factor in life.

Prior to being called to preach, I was an educator. I am heartbroken to see the how today's education system has tried to eliminate Christ from the public classroom. From kindergarten age, where drag queens come and read to the students, to the university setting where students are indoctrinated into liberal philosophies to a Marxist ideology. Despite this climate, there are Christian teachers, along with campus and sport chaplains who make Jesus visible. At the campus in my hometown a number of athletes have had a salvation experience, and they acknowledge Christ as their Lord.

Although numerous liberal, so-called churches dot the landscape of our nation, there is a significant number of x-factor churches who proclaim that "man is a great sinner in need of a great Savior." They believe Jesus is the only way to Heaven (John 14:6) and the Bible is inerrant and trustworthy. A multitude of the people from these churches who have come to Christ, are now serving Jesus locally, nationally, and globally. These are the x-factors because they have a relationship with the X-Factor – Jesus. I baptized two Muslim medical students, and before entering the baptismal water, they wanted me to change their names to John and Mary. They are x-factors by serving the Lord through medicine today in New York City.

In story after story in the gospels, one finds Jesus touching people's lives. The Samaritan lady at the well who was an adulterer or prostitute is an example. Jesus impacted her life by telling her how to quench her thirst (John 4) from having inappropriate relationships. Jesus came to Zacchaeus, the chief tax-collector, in Jericho to impact his life. The deceptive tax-collector believed in Jesus, and he repaid all whom he had cheated by four-fold (Luke 19). The woman caught in adultery was about to be stoned. Jesus asked the Pharisees which of them was without sin to throw the first stone. They departed, and Jesus told the lady that He did not condemn her and to go and sin no more (John 8).

How about you? Has Jesus been the X-Factor for you? It doesn't matter if you claim to be humanistic, secularist, atheist, or however you want to tag yourself, Jesus can impact your life to reveal to you real truth, and real life. All you need to do is to admit to your selfish independent nature and ask Jesus' forgiveness. Pray that Jesus will regenerate your heart like He did mine, and then trust in Jesus' love-work on your behalf through the Cross at Calvary. There on that hill of suffering, Jesus exchanged His righteousness for your sin. In other words, He took upon His body all your sins and credited to your life account righteousness. Through His blood you are justified through your faith and by His grace. Jesus was buried and then on the third day the Father raised Him from the dead. Believe in the death, burial, and bodily resurrection of Jesus, which is the heart of Christianity; this decision allows you to have eternal life, and not to have to face the anguishes of Hell. Jesus' desire is to be your X-Factor of Truth! Come!

Yearning to Give Thanks for Grace

"For it is all for your sake, so that as grace extends to more and
more people it may increase thanksgiving,
to the glory of God" (II Corinthians 4:15).

Paul said that his life is for the sake of others so they might come into a relationship with Jesus. As the gospel spreads to more and more people, these new converts to Christianity give thanks to the glory of God for His grace.

Paul wrote young Timothy that he "suffered or endured for the elect" (2 Timothy 2:10). This means that he yearned for all God's chosen, those who believe the gospel, to experience the saving grace of Jesus Christ. This was Paul's longing mindset to see folks come to salvation.

There was a little lady, four-foot, three-inches, in Southern Baptist life that was a missionary to China for forty-years. Her name was Lottie Moon (1840-1912). Lottie grew up in Albemarle County just outside of Charlottesville, Virginia. She was in a boarding school there – the Albemarle Female Institute a counterpart to the University of Virginia. John Broadus called her, "the most educated woman in the South." Doctor John Broadus was the preacher at First Baptist in Charlottesville where Lottie was born again in 1858, and she was baptized in this church as well. Not long after that, she became engaged to a professor at Southern Seminary by the name of Doctor Toy. But because of his liberal views of Scripture, she broke off the engagement. Soon after the breakup, Lottie began her career as a missionary to China. One of her impressive statements was, "Surely, there is no greater joy than of saving souls." In 1918, Woman's Missionary Union named the annual Christmas offering for international missions after Lottie Moon who urged them to start it. It is no doubt that she had a yearning to see others come to Jesus.

In Colossians 4:2, Paul asked for prayer that doors would be open so the word of the Lord could be declared. Yearning for others to know Christ was always at the forefront of Paul's thinking and prayers. Should we not pray the same as Paul, that the Lord would open doors for us to share the good news of Jesus Christ. When we walk out from our homes, we are entering a mission field. Most do not know Jesus. Pray that opportunities will be available to share the gospel. May we have our Holy Spirit radar on as we journey each day so we can tell others about Jesus.

God's sovereign plan from the beginning was for common folk like us, and the first disciples, mainly fishermen, to carry the gospel forward. As it states in Acts, Peter and John were uneducated men. This really baffled the worldly mature thinkers that such men had so many followers from their message.

According to our text, Paul wanted more people to know Christ so that they would be singing praises of thanksgiving to the Lord. The Pharisees and other religious leaders were evangelists and wanted people to join their faith; they were tithers of their goods; and they were well versed in the Old Testament Scriptures. However, their goal was for their glory and not for the glory of the Lord. No, Paul desired all who followed Jesus to give thanks to the Lord for His glory alone.

One day there will singing and praising the name of Jesus. Revelation 5:13 reads: "And I heard every creature in heaven and on earth and under the earth and in the sea, and all that is in them saying, "To Him who sits on the throne and to the Lamb be blessing and honor and glory and might forever and ever." Revelation 7:9 states, "After this I looked, and behold, a great multitude that no one could number, from every nation, from all tribes and peoples and languages, standing before the throne and before the Lamb clothed in white robes, with palm branches in their hand, and crying out with a loud voice, "Salvation belongs to our God who sits on the throne, and to the Lamb!"

Paul's motivation was to share the gospel, and his yearning was for others to know Jesus so that all would shout praises of thanksgiving to the Lord, now and forever.

Yearning for the Truth

"But it seems that something has happened that has never happened before; though we know not just when, or why, or how, or where. Men have left God not for other gods, they say, but for no gods; and this has never happened before, that men both deny gods and worship gods, professing first Reason, and then money, and power, and what they call life, or race, or dialectic. The church disowned, the tower overthrown, the bells upturned, what have we to do; but stand with empty hands and palms upturned in an age which advances progressively backwards." T.S. Elliot

"As a deer pants for flowing streams, so pants my soul for you, O God. My soul thirsts for God, for the living God . . ." (Psalm 42:1-2a).

The above statements contrast where many Americans are spiritually, some seeking the selfish, independent life, while others are yearning for God. As a nation we live in a dangerous time of America moving "progressively backwards" towards a state of bondage. Alexander Fraser Tytler (1748-1813) wrote about a nation's life cycle. "From bondage to spiritual faith, from spiritual faith to great courage, from great courage to liberty, from liberty to abundance, from abundance to selfishness, from selfishness to complacency, from complacency to dependency, from dependency back to bondage." America has reached the complacency stage which will lead to dependency on the government, which will lead America back to bondage.

What has catapulted our nation into this position of complacency? It is, we as a people of Jesus, who no longer yearn for true-truth. Plus, the complacency condition of our nation is mute from pulpits. The church is to be the pillar of truth (I Timothy 3:15). To overcome his attitude, the Christian must be in the Word of God to understand, and to know how to deal with complacency in their own lives and our nation. I was having dinner with two men who were earning their doctorate degrees in "Biblical Counseling." Our conversation moved to some counseling experiences we have had as pastors. We each agreed that counseling is one of the most arduous tasks in ministry. Why? The majority of counselees do not read the Bible; thus, they don't know the Bible. Consequently, this makes this ministry a monumental task most of the time. Jesus makes it clear what a disciple, follower, and learner of His should be doing:

1. Abiding in the Word - "So Jesus said to the Jews who had believed in Him, "If you abide in My word, you are truly My disciples, and you will know the truth, and the truth will set you free" (John 8:31-32). I believe the abundance we have in America has drawn Christians away from the Bible. We as Christians must battle our way back to abide in the Word. Then, and only then, will we know how to properly manage our abundance, and put our well-being into a biblical perspective.
2. Abandoned life – "Truly, truly, I say to you, unless a grain of wheat falls into the earth and dies, it remains alone; but if it dies, it bears much fruit. Whoever loves his life loses it, and whoever hates his life in this world will keep it for eternal life (John 12:24-25). The church and the Christian can bring correction to our nation by living out what is important in life. Again, if

gaining the world is one's goal, then that will eventually lead to complacency. A life in Christ must be abandoned to Jesus; he must die to the world's glamor and fame. A follower of Jesus proves he is a disciple by seeking the kingdom of God first.

3. Abounds in love – "A new commandment I give to you, that you love one another, just as I have loved you, you also are to love one another. By this all people will know that you are my disciples, if you have love for one another. (John 13:34-35). If people read their Bibles, they know they are to love one another. One of the main problems in the Christian community is unforgiveness. We are not showing others that we truly follow Christ if we have an unforgiving attitude.

4. Abundant fruit is produced – "By this my Father is glorified, that you bear much fruit and so prove to be my disciple (John 15:8). Fruit bearing is multicolored. Inevitably, the Christian produces fruit. It is just a part of who he is through the Holy Spirit. He produces one fruit with nine characteristics in the believer: joy, love, peace, etc. (Galatians 5:22-23). This fruit is to be displayed in the Christian's life towards others. But also, He creates ministry fruit as well (I Corinthians 12:11). Each believer receives gifts for ministry. These fruits of the Holy Spirit when allowed to exercise can bring change to America.

Jesus taught the priority of life, "But seek first the kingdom of God and his righteousness, and all these things will be added to you" (Matthew 6:33). Proverbs 14:34f reads, "Righteousness exalts a nation, but sin is a disgrace to any people." Jesus is saying for us to thirst for, yearn for, His righteousness and to be in a right relationship with Him. The yearning is towards the person who can teach the Truth, not a truth. Unless we reprioritize our lives, we will be a people wandering in the wilderness, thinking, "How did we get to this place?"

Listen carefully! Jesus' teachings will set you free. As He stated, if we seek Him first, He will provide, care, and protect us. On the other end of the spectrum, people clamor for the government to be the provider, caretaker, and protector. That comes with a price. The price tag is higher taxes, politically correct mandatory speech, and allegiance to the government, not God. In Nazi Germany in 1935, prayers ceased in schools; only state approved teachers taught religion; doctrines of the Bible were replaced for the dogmas of Nazism; Christmas and Easter changed to 'Yuletide' and 'arrival of spring;" the swastikas replaced the cross and other symbols of the Christian church. Listen to Hitler, "Do you really believe the masses will be Christian again? Nonsense! Never again. That tale is finished. No one will listen to it again. Even the pastors will support us."

Unless our nation, especially the church, yearns for Jesus – the Truth, we will find ourselves back in a 1935 of bondage. We must pull away from our complacent attitude. We must first seek God's authority in our lives and a right relationship with the Lord, then He will bring peace. But if we continue towards universal income, health care, and education, the socialist voices will have successfully removed God from America.

Are you yearning for the God of Truth? Do you thirst for the living God who gives us living truth- the Scriptures? "Blessed are those who hunger and thirst after righteousness, for they shall be satisfied" (Matthew 5:6).

ZENITH OF GRACE IS JESUS

"And the Word became flesh and dwelt among us, and we have seen His glory, glory as of the only Son from the Father, full of grace and truth" (John 1:14).

"For the law was given through Moses; grace and truth came through Jesus Christ" (John 1:17).

According to the *Oxford Dictionary*, "Zenith is the time something is most powerful or successful." Grace is the most powerful and successful because God came in the person of His Son – Jesus. Jesus is "the radiance of the glory of God and the exact imprint of His nature, and He upholds the universe by the word of His power" (Hebrews 1:3). Grace was manifested through Jesus throughout His thirty-three years on earth. Time and time again, He displayed grace either by healing someone, feeding a multitude, calming a storm; but grace was magnified when He granted salvation to a host of people.

My wife and I went on a sabbatical to Colorado. While there, we took the cog train to the top of Pike's Peak Mountain. From a distance we could see this 14,115-foot mountain. It was magnificent. But until we ascended the mountain, we could not experience the beauty and awesomeness of the mountain. At ground level the temperature was sixty degrees. Once atop Pike's Peak, the temperature was thirty-three degrees, and we could see for miles. In fact, we could see four states.

When grace intervenes in your life, you have a Pike's Peak experience. You see the world differently. Jesus is full of grace and grace came through Him. If you don't have Jesus in your life, you will never understand grace, nor will you experience the true reality of life.

Being yoked to Jesus allows grace to unlock life's blessings for the believer. Unless one is yoked to Jesus, he will always carry the weight of sin in his mind and life. When receiving salvation, you are forgiven of all your sins. Then you understand that you are to forgive others of their sins. Grace was given to the believer and the believer is to grant grace to those who offend him.

Jesus is clear in Matthew 11:28-30, that His yoke is easy and His burden is light. A yoke was worn by two oxen that would divide the weight of pulling a wagon. Jesus is saying for us to be hooked to Him, to walk with Him side-by-side, and He will give us rest for our souls. This picture of being yoked is a prime illustration of the Lord's grace upon our lives.

Jesus is "full" of grace. That is, He is overflows with grace. Paul makes this crystal clear in his theological letter to the Romans. In 5:20b he writes, "But where sin abounded, grace abounded much more" (NKJV). The ESV says, ". . . but where sin increased, grace abounded all the more." The *Amplified Bible* states, "But where sin increased, [God's remarkable, gracious gift of] grace [His unmerited favor] has surpassed it and increased all the more, . . ."

Jesus is the embodiment of grace. He overflows with the gift of grace to all who call on His name to be saved, which brings them into a relationship with Jesus. He grants hope, rest, peace, and joy to all who have confessed Him as Lord. We have hope for the guarantee of a future home in heaven. Rest in Jesus in the trials of life, and experience peace that passes all understanding, for there is peace with God (Romans 5:1) and the peace of God (Philippians 4:7) in life. Peace with God is that His wrath is no longer an issue in our lives. Peace of God is that He provides satisfaction in life. Each aspect of peace is a run-off of His grace towards us.

Life is tough, full of trials and temptations, and then we die. In the midst of the trials and temptations, we know that Jesus is there with us. In Daniel 3, He was with Shadrach, Meshach, and Abed-Nego in the fiery furnace of Nebuchadnezzar. He was with Peter and John in prison as recorded by Doctor Luke in Acts 4. Also, He was with Paul through his beatings, shipwrecks, survival of a stoning, the perils of false brethren, and much more (2 Corinthians 11: 22-33).

All these biblical examples are given to us so that we might know that Jesus is with us. His grace comforts us knowing that the One who is full of grace is there with us in our fiery moments of life, in our seeming defeats in life, and through the unfairness's we go through in life.

Praise the Lord, for He is with us and His grace sustains us, satisfies us, and allows our lives to bring glory and honor to the King of kings and Lord of lords.

Jesus is the zenith of life because He comes in a person's life to regenerate him by giving grace, but also to overflow the person with grace daily. Jesus is the most powerful in making a tsunami of grace the most prominent aspect of a person's life.

ZENITH OF THE TRUTH IS THE RESURRECTION

"Now if Christ is proclaimed as raised from the dead, how can some of you say that there is no resurrection of the dead? But if there is no resurrection of the dead, then not even Christ has been raised. And if Christ has not been raised, then our preaching is in vain and your faith is in vain. We are even found to be misrepresenting God, because we testified about God that he raised Christ, whom he did not raise if it is true that the dead are not raised. For if the dead are not raised, not even Christ has been raised. And if Christ has not been raised, your faith is futile and you are still in your sins. Then those also who have fallen asleep in Christ have perished. If in Christ we have hope in this life only, we are of all people most to be pitied" (I Corinthians 15:12-19).

"If you discount the resurrection, then you have a hard time explaining how the Christian church got stared in the first place." Timothy Keller

As stated before, Zenith defined by the *Oxford Dictionary* is "the time at which something is most powerful or successful." The most fruitful moment or powerful time in Jesus' ministry was when the tomb was empty. Yes, the Cross is highly significant in the Christian faith. However, without the resurrection of Jesus, the Cross would be insignificant. This is why the resurrection is the zenith of truth. The resurrection of Jesus fulfills all the promises of Scripture, the teachings of Jesus, and the future of the church. The apostle Paul stated in the focus text, that without the resurrection our faith is meaningless and preaching is pointless. Still more important, everyone will still live in their sinful nature.

As I've written throughout the book, the sun has set on America and most people are living in darkness. The sinful nature creates darkness in a person's life. Paul describes in Romans 1: 18 – Romans 3 the depth of depravity in humanity. The Apostle of grace shares that the souls of humankind are in darkness, they are fools, ignorant, prideful, they are just living for their own pleasures. Then in the Roman's text, Paul tells how most worship the creature instead of the Creator; how the now find pleasure in homosexual acts. God has "given them up" in their sinful nature. Yes, they know about God from the general revelation about God. However, they don't have God's special revelation of sovereign grace for salvation. Consequently, they live in unrighteousness. To remove the darkness, they must be called by God for salvation. Then a tsunami of grace and truth will flow over their hearts so an understanding of the resurrection of Jesus Christ can be achieved.

Yes, the resurrection is the heart of Christianity. It is the most powerful moment in history. Of all the faiths in the world, Jesus is the only and true God who is living. All human gods are lifeless. However, the Christian worships a living God, who has given His living Word, the Bible, (Hebrews 4:12), and Who has granted a living hope for all who believe in His death, burial, and resurrection according to the scriptures (I Corinthians 15:3-4).

Jesus' resurrection solidifies the Truth. The historical event is the glue that holds truth together. John writes in his second letter, "for the sake of the truth which abides in us and will be with us forever:" (2 John 2). He wrote the epistle for "truth" that the reader would not compromise the truth. The reason the "truth abides in us" is because a believer has the Spirit of truth, the Holy Spirit, living in him. The reason the Holy Spirit can live in a Christian is because of the resurrection of Jesus (John 16:7). Jesus told His disciples that if He didn't go away the Helper would not come (John 16:7). The Paraclete, the Holy Spirit, will come to live within and walk with the believer. The Spirit of truth will always be with the believer.

There are basically three choices about life after death. One, there is no life after death. The life one now lives is it. I have relatives who hold to this belief. How sad to think they believe that their current life will just end with no future. One day they will see truth when they stand before the Lord. Second, reincarnation is a popular belief today. One's soul returns to the earth as another person. Many embrace this idea. Most in this arena of belief are in the Eastern religious faiths, like Buddhism. Third, is the resurrection. Like Jesus, a believer will have a bodily resurrection. The resurrected body will be recognizable, incorruptible, and glorified.

Which of the three after death experiences is true? Which do you hold fast to?

Actually, the resurrection is the only one that can be validated because history agrees that Jesus' tomb was vacant after He was buried. The swoon theory (Jesus was drugged), the twin theory (Jesus had a twin), and other weightless theories try to disprove Jesus' resurrection, but have failed wretchedly. However, a leading authority on the study of the resurrection, Dr. Gary Habermas weighs in on the discussion. He asks two questions: Did Jesus die and was Jesus later seen alive? Well, history proves He died. He was whipped with at least thirty-nine lashes causing his flesh to be ripped from His body. His torn body had to carry part of His cross to Calvary's Hill. Then He was crucified. Three nails were driven into His body, one in each wrist, and a third

Zenith of the Truth is the Resurrection

through His ankles. As He was dying, a Roman guard thrusted a spear into His side. After taking His last breath, His body was removed and then buried in a borrowed tomb. Georgia Tech University engineers estimate that the stone rolled in front of the tomb was at least two tons. Yes, He died. To be sure Jesus died and He was buried, Pilate placed a guard of twelve men in front of the tomb, and he sealed the tomb with a cord with his signet ring imprint on the seal. But was He seen after He was buried? Yes! There were at least five hundred eyewitnesses that saw Him (I Corinthians 15:5). It was witnessed that Jesus came to His disciples where Thomas had to see and touch His hands and side (John 20:24-25). In the same text, the disciples heard, saw, and touched Jesus. But what is really far reaching is what Keller asked, how would the church have started, and how has the church continued through so many centuries if there was no resurrection?

The resurrection is indeed the highwater mark in history, the most powerful moment in history. It is indeed a zenith of truth surrounding Jesus Christ. All true-truth hinges on this one historical event.

I ask: Where are you finding truth? Most non-believers are gleaning truth from politicians, liberal clergy (who only believe the Bible contains truth), the media, from their own opinion or experience, or from a non-Christian faith? Believers find truth and live truth from Scripture whose Author is Jesus Christ. Come to Jesus, the risen Lord, and He will teach you the truth that will set you free. Yes, Jesus will and can send a tsunami of grace and truth over your life which will deliver you from darkness into His glorious light.

"AMEN AND AMEN!"

EPILOGUE

I believe you understand, after reading this, why I claim the sun has set on America and most people are living in darkness. The antidote for the darkness is a tsunami of grace and truth. But grace and truth can only come from the One who is full of grace and truth – Jesus. Grace and truth come to life in a person when the light of Jesus shines on them. Jesus said, "I am the light of the world. Whoever follows Me will not walk in darkness, but will have the light of life" (John 8:12).

Darkness is simply the absence of light. In our house, the guest bathroom has a night light. When we enter the house at night, the night light pushes back enough darkness so I can turn another light on. However, Jesus is the eternal light, and He eliminates darkness. His rays are such they would blind you. You probably have driven when the sun hinders your driving ability. The sun rays are so incredibly intense. Think of Jesus' light as a blinding light. Like the Apostle Paul experienced on the Damascus road, a flash of light from heaven truly made him blind.

The light of Jesus enlightens the heart so that our eyes are open to see truth. When you are born again, then the light of Jesus allows you to see the broad road you are traveling on to enter through a wide gate that leads to Hell. Jesus' light will lead you to a narrow road and gate,

Epilogue

and that way is hard, and only a few find it (Matthew 7:13-14). David in Psalm 23:3 calls this path, a path of righteousness, a path leading to heaven.

To take a stand against abortion, transgenderism, socialism, green energy, open boarders, etc. is the narrow road and gate. All those who support the list are on the broad road that leads to destruction and there are many on this road. But the light of Jesus reveals how dark such beliefs are. As I said, the sun has set on America, and most are settling in darkness. The light of Jesus will not only push back the darkness but eradicate it as well. Then you see how grace and truth wash over your heart to see truth.

Grace is when someone gets a "do over." And there can be numerous do overs. For example, those who have an abortion can experience God's grace to bring peace to your guilt and He will restore you. My prayer is God will send such a skyscraper of a tsunami of grace and truth that revival breaks out across America. That all the sinful woes of America will be forgiven. People will acknowledge that God is in control of their lives and this nation. I don't believe God is finished with or has given up on America. By His grace and mercy, we will have the light of life again.

NOTES

Introduction

https.wwwgoodreads.com – Dietrich Bonhoeffer

https.wwwbrainyquote.com - inspirational quotes by Hiram Johnson

Abounding Grace

Absoluteness of the Truth

Oz Guinness, *Time for Truth: Living free in a world of Lies, Hype, and Spin;* (Grand Rapids, Michigan, Baker Books, 2000), p.82.

Nancy Pearcey, *Total Truth: Liberating Christianity from It's Cultural Captivity*; (Wheaton, Illinois, Crossway Books, 2004), p.16.

Building Upon the Word of Grace

The Bible is the Truth

Nancy Pearcey, *Total Truth: Liberating Christianity from Its Cultural Captivity*; (Wheaton, Illinois, Crossway Books, 2004), p.33.

R. Albert Mohler, Jr., *Feed My Sheep: A Passionate Plea for Preaching: The Primacy of Preaching*; (Orlando, Florida, Reformation Trust Publishing, 2008), p.10.

Notes

Common Grace

Church – The Upholder of "True-Truth"
https://www.thegospelcoalition.org: Be Where the Battle Rages

Drawn to the Throne of Grace
C.S. Lewis, *The Problem of Pain*; (New York, New York, HarperCollins Publishers, 1996)

https://www.desiringgod.org, "Let's Find "Grace for a Well-Timed Help" Together," November 17, 1993.

Discovering the Truth
Saint Augustine, *The Confessions*, (New York, New York, Penguin Random House,

Equipped for Ministry by Grace

Evaporation of the Truth
Oz Guinness, *Time for Truth: Living free in a world of Lies, Hype, and Spin;* (Grand Rapids, Michigan, Baker Books, 2000), p.19.

Ibid. p. 19.

Free Gift of Jesus through Grace

Freedom in Truth
Oz Guinness, *Time for Truth: Living free in a world of Lies, Hype, and Spin;* (Grand Rapids, Michigan, Baker Books, 2000), p.87.

Ibid., p.86.

God of All Grace
Kenneth S. Wuest, https://www.preceptaustin.org, I Peter 5:10.

God of the Truth

Humbleness Receives Greater Grace
Andrew Murray, *Humility: The Beauty of Holiness*; (Washington, Pennsylvania, Christian Literature Crusade, 1896), p.42.

John Calvin, *Institutes*; (Philadelphia, Pennsylvania, Presbyterian Board of Publication and Sabbath School Work, 1921), Volume 1, 2.2.11.

Holy Spirit of the Truth
Francis Chan, *Forgotten God: Reversing Our Tragic Neglect of the Holy Spirit;* (Colorado Springs, Colorado, David Cook Publishers, 2009, p.20.

Ibid. p.14

Identity from Grace

Indoctrination in the Truth
Https://www.baptistnews.com: Falwell and Luther: a theology of glory verses a theology of the Cross.

https://www.goodreads.com – Newton

Justified by Grace
Wayne Grudem, *Systematic Theology: An Introduction to Biblical Doctrine*, (Grand Rapids, Michigan, Zondervan, 1994). p.1246.

Joy in the Truth
Joe Holland's article in, "Table Talk," February, 2017.

Koinonia (Fellowship) from Grace

Knowledge of the Truth
Https://www.goodreads.com: Luther on Reason.

Notes

Law Submits to Grace

Lack of the Truth

Multiplication of Grace
"Precept Austin," website, 2 Peter 2:2.

Never Nullify the Grace of God
https://www.leslieleylandfields.com, "Let the Stable Still Astonish."

Nation of Truth
Oz Guinness, *Time for Truth: Living free in a world of Lies, Hype, and Spin;* (Grand Rapids, Michigan, Baker Books, 2000), pgs. 78,79,80.

Ibid., p.78.

Only by Grace is Someone Born Again

Overcomers for the Truth

Presence of God at the Throne of Grace
Vincent, Word Studies in NT, vol. 4, p.109.

htts://www.azquotes, Donald Barnhouse Quotes.

https://www.desiringgod.org, "Let's Find "Grace for a Well-Timed Help" Together," November 17, 1993.

Daniel Henderson, *21 Days of Transforming Prayer*: (Denver Colorado, Strategic Renewal, 2021), p.14.

Practice of the Truth

Qualified to Preach the Grace of God

Quandary Around the Truth

C. S. Lewis, *Mere Christianity*, (San Francisco, Harper, 1952, republished 20001), p. 55-56.

C.S. Lewis, *The Chronicles of Narnia, Book Six, The Silver Chair*, (New York, New York, HarperTrophy Publishers, 1953, republished 2000).

Riches of God's Grace

Reconstruction of the Truth

Oz Guinness, *Time for Truth: Living free in a world of Lies, Hype, and Spin;* (Grand Rapids, Michigan, Baker Books, 2000), p.56.

https://www.throughtout history.com: story of the Brooklyn Bridge.

Francis Frangipane, *Holiness, Truth and the Presence of God*, (Lake Mary, Florida, Charisma House, 2011), p. 2.

Sufficiency of God's Grace

Mrs. C.H. Morris, *Eternal Praise Hymnal: His Grace is Sufficient for Me* (Chicago, Illinois, Hope Publishing Company,1918), p.118.

Suffering for the Truth

https://www.christianitytoday.com: December 4, 2014, "Sorry, Tertullian."

https://www.goodreads.com: J.C. Ryle, English Anglican Bishop of Liverpool, 2024.

https://www.christianhistoryinstitute.org: Polycarp testimony.

https://www.apostolic.edu. Don McAlvany, *The Midnight Herald*, "Persecution of Christians Growing in the United States," May 13, 2009.

Testifying to the Gospel of God's Grace

Notes

Tolerance of the Truth

Nancy Pearcy, *Total Truth: Liberating Christianity from Its Cultural Captivity*, (Wheaton, Illinois, Crossway Books, 2004).

John MacArthur, *The Truth War: Fighting for Christianity in an Age of Deception*, (Nashville, Tennessee, Thomas Nelson Books, 2007).

Oz Guinness, *Time for Truth: Living free in a world of Lies, Hype, and Spin;* (Grand Rapids, Michigan, Baker Books, 2000), p.84.

Ibid., p. 84.

Charles Colson, *The Good Life*, (Wheaton, Illinois, Tyndale House Publishers, Inc., 2005), p. 225.

https://www.wordsofgrace.blog. (John MacArthur, "Lies We Believe," May 11, 2007).

Unity in the Church Through Grace

Larry W. Osborne, *The Unity Factor*, (Vista, California, Owls Nest Publishers, 2006), p.10.

Marty Lloyd-Jones, *Ephesians Commentary 4:1-16: Christian Unity*, (Grand Rapids, Michigan, Baker Books, 1980), p.24-26.

Universality of the Truth

Oz Guinness, *Time for Truth: Living free in a world of Lies, Hype, and Spin;* (Grand Rapids, Michigan, Baker Books, 2000), p.19.

https://www.reddit.com: movies.

https://www.dukehealth.org – blog, "9 Signs of Narcissistic Personality Disorder," December 15, 2022.

Victory in the Future by Grace

Sallie Martin, *Eternal Praise Hymnal: His Grace is Sufficient for Me* (Chicago, Illinois, Hope Publishing Company,1918), p.76.

Voice of Truth

Charles Colson, *The Good Life*, (Wheaton, Illinois, Tyndale House Publishers, Inc., 2005), p. 197.

Oz Guinness, *Time for Truth: Living free in a world of Lies, Hype, and Spin;* (Grand Rapids, Michigan, Baker Books, 2000), p.81.

Wisdom from the Grace of God

https://www.goodreads.com: Bonhoeffer.

https://www.brainyquote.com: Martin Luther.

Dietrich Bonhoeffer, *The Cost of Discipleship*, (New York, New York, Simon & Schuster, 1995), p.60

Weight of Truth

Oz Guinness, *Time for Truth: Living free in a world of Lies, Hype, and Spin;* (Grand Rapids, Michigan, Baker Books, 2000), p.11.

Ibid. p. 14.

https://www.actoninstitute.org – Horace Mann

https://www.answersingensis.org – The Failure of John Dewy

https://www.antoniogramsci.com: quotes on socialism.

X-Factor in Christianity is Grace

X-Factor of the Truth

Yearning to Give Thanks for Grace

Yearning for the Truth

https://www.quotefancy.com: T.S. Elliot

https://www.commonsensegovernment.com: Tytler

https://www.books.google.com: Hitler

Notes

Zenith of Grace is Jesus

Zenith of the Truth is the Resurrection
https://www.thegospelcoalition.org. 20 Quotes from Tim Keller on Resurrection Hope.

www.ingramcontent.com/pod-product-compliance
Lightning Source LLC
LaVergne TN
LVHW091534070526
838199LV00001B/57